BUDDHISM

VOLUME ONE—HINAYANA

BUDDHISM

VOLUME ONE—HINAYANA

By

C. H. S. WARD

THE EPWORTH PRESS

(EDGAR C. BARTON)

25-35 CITY ROAD, LONDON, E.C.1

First published (as *Outline of Buddhism*), 1934
This (Revised) edition, 1947

MADE AND PRINTED IN GREAT BRITAIN
BY PURNELL AND SONS LTD., PAULTON (SOMERSET) AND LONDON

PREFACE TO REVISED EDITION

THIS BOOK was written to meet a felt need for a book on Buddhism, at once modern, scholarly, concise, and comprehensive. Though meant primarily for students, its clear style and simplicity of language should make it interesting to the general reader, and give him a real insight into the culture and fundamental outlook of the Buddhist peoples of Ceylon, Burma, and Siam.

The whole ground of *Hīnayāna* Buddhism is covered in this book, and it is fully documented. It also contains an Index of Names, and an Index of Subjects, which enable the student easily to follow up any subject on which he requires fuller information.

When the first edition was sold out, the Editor of the Series, and the Publishers, wished to reprint it, but difficulties in the printing and publishing trades have delayed the reissue until now.

The book has been carefully revised. Particular attention has been paid to the Indexes to make them fuller and more comprehensive. Sanskrit and Pali words in the Indexes have been accented, so that the reader may know how to pronounce them.

The author has been asked to write a second volume for this Series on *Mahāyāna* Buddhism, which will supplement the present book.

In the new volume, which will be published as soon as possible, knowledge of this one will be assumed, and it is hoped by means of cross references to avoid as far as possible detailed discussions of subjects already dealt with in Volume One, and make possible a fuller and more detailed treatment of *Mahāyāna* Buddhism.

The two volumes are intended to cover the whole ground of Buddhism in all its varieties and stages of development. Together they should give the student at least a foundation of sound knowledge on which he will be able to build with confidence.

1947.   C.H.S.W.

EDITOR'S FOREWORD

THE quest for God is one in which all nations have shared. Call Him what they may, all peoples seek God, though they seek not as do we. Yet to understand both their unity with and differences from us must help to closer sympathy and respect. The purpose of this series is not critical nor apologetic, but rather is it descriptive. It is that of giving some account, by reference to the Scriptures and great teachers of other religions, of the way in which the faiths of the world have faced the same spiritual issues that are ours. In this respect they are intended as a simply written contribution to the work of the Comparative Study of Religions.

E.S.W.

CONTENTS

		PAGE
PREFACE TO REVISED EDITION	. . .	5
EDITOR'S FOREWORD	. . . . .	6
INTRODUCTION	. . . . .	9

PART I

I.	THE SOURCES OF OUR KNOWLEDGE OF THE BUDDHA AND HIS TEACHING . . .	15
II.	THE BUDDHA	23
III.	THE BIRTH AND EARLY LIFE OF GOTAMA BUDDHA	26
IV.	THE 'HOME LEAVING' OF GOTAMA BUDDHA	30
V.	THE PUBLIC MINISTRY OF GOTAMA BUDDHA	43
VI.	THE LAST WORDS AND DEATH OF GOTAMA BUDDHA	49

PART II

VII.	BUDDHIST DOCTRINE: ITS ETHICS, PSYCHOLOGY AND METAPHYSICS	61
VIII.	THE THREE UNIVERSAL TRUTHS . . .	66
IX.	THE BUDDHIST DOCTRINE OF MAN . .	71
X.	KARMA AND REBIRTH, OR THE BUDDHA'S TEACHING ABOUT THE FUTURE LIFE . .	83
XI.	THE BUDDHA'S WAY OF SALVATION. NIRVANA: WHAT IT IS, AND HOW IT IS TO BE ATTAINED	95

PART III

		PAGE
XII.	THE ORDER OF THE BUDDHA'S DISCIPLES .	111
XIII.	THE HISTORICAL DEVELOPMENT OF BUDDHISM	119
XIV.	BUDDHISM AS A RELIGION	123

APPENDIX I

	LITERATURE	130
I.	THE BUDDHA AND HIS DOCTRINE . . .	130
II.	TRANSLATIONS FROM THE BUDDHIST *Canon* AND OTHER AUTHORITATIVE *Pali* BOOKS	132
III.	MISCELLANEOUS LITERATURE. . . .	133

APPENDIX II

INDEX OF NAMES	135

APPENDIX III

INDEX OF SUBJECTS	139

INTRODUCTION

WHEN WRITING about Buddhism, which has developed along so many and various lines, it is necessary to state clearly, at the very outset, with what kind of Buddhism we are going to deal. For the purposes of this study we shall accept as Buddhism nothing that is not actually found in the *Pali Pitakas*, or is clearly deducible from them.

This rule will exclude some of the most distinctive doctrines of the great *Mahayana* School of Buddhism. Nevertheless, we wish to avoid even the suspicion of undervaluing Mahayana Buddhism as a religion, for it is the faith of the overwhelming majority of living Buddhists, and their claim that it possesses a religious value for mankind superior to that of *Hinayana* Buddhism can, probably, be made good. The fact remains, however, that there is very little left in the Mahayana teaching that the Buddha would have recognized or acknowledged as his.

For example, the Mahayanists deny that the Buddha ever possessed a material body, or was in any real sense a man, or that he really entered Nirvana. ' Sakyamuni did not appear in person in the world, but deputed an image of himself to represent him.'[1]

Moreover, in the Mahayana, ' the Buddhas from the first are nothing but divine beings, and their peregrinations on the earth, and their entry into Nirvana, no more than a freak or thoughtless play.' The Mahayana, while regarding the Ideal Buddha as the Supreme and Eternal God, counts its Buddhas by millions, and ' Hindu gods and goddesses, especially of the *Shiva* Cycle, are placed on a

[1] L. De La Vallee Poussin in *E.R.E.*, Vol. I, pp. 95-96.

par with the Buddhas and Bodhisattvas, and contribute to the amplification of the Buddhist pantheon.'[1]

'Further, we must admit, however reluctantly, that the masses of Asia, who have seen in the Buddha the Light of the World, have not done so because of his rationalistic doctrines, his chain of causation, which they have understood as little as do we, or even his advice to still passion. They have adored him as the God of Gods, and believed that by devotion to him they shall attain eternal salvation, consisting of perpetual bliss.'[2]

Contrast with the above quotations the statements of two Hinayana Buddhist Monks. Writing on the Buddha and Buddhism, the first says : ' The position which Buddhism occupies among religions is one wholly unique. The great mass of the religions of the world is founded on some sort of revelation from a supra-human, supernatural source. This religion, on the contrary, is the outcome pure and simple of the strenuous mental and spiritual effort, continued through many years of a human being unhelped by any outward aid.[3]

The second quotation is from a little book entitled *Buddhism in a Nutshell*, by Bhikkhu Narada, published in Ceylon in October 1933. This young monk was educated in an English High School, and is looked up to as a leader by the educated Buddhist young men and boys of Ceylon. In this book p. 3, he writes :

' The Buddha was, therefore, a human being. As a man He was born, as a man He lived, and as a man His life came to an end. Though a human being, He became an extraordinary man—*Acchariya Manussa*—as He himself says in the *Anguttara-Nikaya*. The Buddha laid stress on this

---

[1] *Literary History of Sanskrit Buddhism*, by G. K. Nariman, p. 5. Published by Indian Book Depot, Bombay.
[2] *Buddhist Philosophy*, by A. B. Keith, D.C.L., D.Litt., pp. 14-15.
[3] Silacara Bhikkhu, *Lotus Blossoms*, p. 2. Theosophical Publishing House, Adyar, Madras.

important point and left no room whatever to transform Himself to the state of an immortal divine being.'

'Neither does He claim to be an incarnation of Vishnu, as the Hindus are apt to believe, nor does He call Himself a saviour who saves others by His personal salvation. The Buddha exhorts His disciples to depend on themselves for their salvation, for both purity and defilement depend on oneself. In the *Dhammapada* He says—"*Tumhehi kiccan ātappan—Akkhātāro Tathāgatā.*" You yourselves should make the exertion, the *Tathāgatās* are only teachers.'

'The Buddhas point out the path, and it is left for us to follow that path to save ourselves.'

'To depend on others for salvation is negative, but to depend on oneself is positive.'

'In exhorting His disciples to be self-dependent the Buddha says in the *Parinibbana-Sutta* :—"Be ye islands unto yourselves, be ye a refuge unto yourselves, seek not for refuge in others."'

This fairly represents the position held by intelligent Buddhists of the *Hinayana* School. It will be clear to every reader, I think, that the beliefs of the two great Schools of Buddhists cannot be harmonized, but that they must be treated quite independently and separately.

One other aspect of Buddhism must be mentioned. Mrs. C. A. F. Rhys Davids, during the last few years, has been calling upon Buddhists to forsake the 'monkish' teaching of Buddhism, which has dominated them at least from the time when the *Pitakas* were edited and reduced to writing, and to return to the *primitive* teachings of Sakyamuni, which she believes can be recovered from the Pali books.

Mrs. Rhys Davids has brought ripe scholarship, and a wide and profound knowledge of the original sources, to the task. Her reconstruction of Buddhism is fundamental, and deals especially with those doctrines which are regarded as essential by Buddhists of all Schools.

She has given the results of her investigations in a series of books which total 1,500 or more pages of printed matter, and it would be an impertinence to attempt to summarize that teaching in the space at my disposal. I can only refer the reader to her own books, and especially to *Gotama the Man*, and *Sakya*.

Whilst writing this book, I have continually kept in mind the needs of the busy student and the general reader, who might have neither time nor opportunity to consult many books. Therefore, instead of merely giving references to important passages, I have quoted the actual words as far as possible.

This has sometimes led to a drastic curtailment of what I myself had written. But, in a book of this size on so large a subject, severe selection is unavoidable.

PART I

I

THE SOURCES OF OUR KNOWLEDGE OF
THE BUDDHA AND HIS TEACHING

Since we are separated from the Buddha by twenty-four centuries, it is of the most vital importance to estimate at their true value the sources of our knowledge of him and his teaching.

These sources are the *Pali Pitakas*, for, though there are other books of great value to Buddhism, such as the ancient Pali Commentaries on the *Pitakas*, *The Milinda-panha* (or 'The Questions of King Milinda'), *The Visuddhimagga* (or 'The Path of Purity'), and many others, they are all dependent upon the *Tripitaka* as Christian Literature is dependent upon the Bible. The *Tripitaka* has a value for *Hinayana* Buddhism comparable to that of the New Testament for Christianity, and the Quran for Islam.

The Buddhist *Canon* consists of three collections of texts, termed *Tripitaka*, or 'Triple Basket.' *Pali*, the language in which they are written, is a post Asokan artificial literary language, of the origin of which we have no certain knowledge. So complex is the problem that the greatest Pali scholars are unable to arrive at a common solution, and Oldenberg, Rhys Davids, Franke, Grierson, Geiger, Levi, Keith, Turner, to mention no more, each has a theory of his own. While the experts disagree we must suspend our judgement. 'The obvious deduction is that Pali came into being, such as we have it, by a slow and complex process occupying centuries, and variations of place.'[1]

[1] Keith, *Buddhist Philosophy*, pp. 24, 25.   See also Mrs. Rhys Davids, *Sakya*, pp. 24-25, and 429-30.

The *Pali Tripitaka* is divided into (1) the *Vinaya-Pitaka*, (2) the *Sutta-Pitaka*, and (3) the *Abhidhamma-Pitaka*.

The *Vinaya* consists chiefly of the rules and regulations for the life and behaviour of the Buddhist monks and nuns.

The *Sutta* contains statements of Buddhist faith, speculations, and philosophical theories, together with sermons and conversations supposed to be in the very words of the Buddha.

The *Abhidhamma* is made up of supplementary treatises dealing with controverted points of doctrine and practice, enlarging upon and making additions to the earlier Pitakas.[1]

The Vinaya-Pitaka is divided into three sections :

I	*Khandhakas* :
	  (i) Mahavagga
	  (ii) Cullavagga
		These texts give a detailed code of duties to be performed by monks and nuns. The Cullavagga also contains a history of the Councils supposed to have been summoned after the death of the Buddha.

II	*Sutta-Vibhanga* :
	  (i) Patimokkha
	  (ii) Commentary
	  on Patimokkha
		Chiefly a catalogue of sins and regulations pertaining to them. This was intended to be publicly read on the days of confession.

III	*Parivara* :	A concise summary of the other books.

The Sutta-Pitaka is divided into five sections :

I	*Digha-Nikaya* :	This is composed of the longest texts, thirty-four in number. (Digha=long.)
II	*Majjhima-Nikaya* :	A collection of texts of medium length. (Majjhima=medium.)
III	*Samyutta-Nikaya* :	A collection of various kinds of sayings.
IV	*Anguttara-Nikaya* :	In which the texts relating to numerical rubrics are gathered together and classified in ascending order.

[1] See Geden, *Studies in Eastern Religions*, pp. 237-39.

V *Khuddaka-Nikaya* :	This is called the minor collection, and gathers up all the texts which have not been included in the previous collections. It is clearly inferior to the other four, and includes not only ' The Word of the Buddha,' but also works nominally attributed to disciples of the Buddha. It includes the *Dhammapada*, and the *Jataka*.
The Abhidhamma-Pitaka.	This *Pitaka* is much later in date than the *Vinaya* and the *Sutta Pitakas*, and consists of seven books of Metaphysics :

I	Dhamma sangani.	V	Katha vatthu.
II	Vibhanga.	VI	Yamaka.
III	Dhatukatha.	VII	Patthana.
IV	Puggala pannatti.		

The Buddha (like Jesus), left behind him no written works, but immediately after his death, according to orthodox Buddhist tradition, a great Council of 500 monks came together at Rajagaha (modern Rajgar) and ' Upali and Ananda rehearsed respectively the Vinaya and Dhamma. Thus the authorized version of the sayings of the Master was established and fixed.' No mention is made here of the Abhidhamma, the third division, which, with the Vinaya and the Dhamma, completes the Buddhist Canon.

A hundred years later, a second general Council is said to have been held at Vaisali to settle ten questions of monastic discipline, which were exercising the community, and ' to pronounce upon the lawfulness or otherwise of certain relaxations of strict rule which had been adopted by a party among the monks.' To this Council was given the name of *Mahasangiti*, or ' Great Council ' ; and here, as at Rajagaha, the Vinaya and Dhamma were rehearsed, no mention being made of the Abhidhamma.

The Council of Pataliputta is said to have been held, under the patronage of King Asoka, and under the presidency of his deputy, the distinguished monk, Tissa, about a century after Vaisali, ' for the uprooting and destruction of all false doctrine,' because the Buddhist community was, at that time, rent by schisms.

The Council of Kanishka was held about A.D. 100, but of the details of the Council nothing is known.[1]

What value have these Councils for the fixing of the date of the *Canon*, and as evidence for the genuineness of its books ? It is hard to say. Some scholars suggest that the first three Councils are but names without historical reality. The probability is, and we cannot get farther than probability at present, that soon after the death of the Buddha, his chief disciples gathered together in council, and endeavoured to summarize his teaching, the substance of which, according to the custom of the age, would have been memorized by one or other of his followers. In course of time the traditional teaching became corrupted and heresies arose—we have evidence of this—and efforts would be made to free the *Primitive Doctrine* from the later additions. Therefore, whether the *traditional* Councils are historical or not, is, for the present discussion, of no great importance, since councils for the same purpose must have been held.

It is of the most vital importance for us, however, to find out, as nearly as possible, with what degree of faithfulness our Pitakas set forth the life, the character, and the teaching of the Buddha.

The art of writing was known, but very little practised for the writing of books, in the India of early Buddhism, and it is acknowledged by all, that the Pitakas were not reduced to writing until long after the Buddha's death.

[1] See Geden, *Studies in Eastern Religions*, pp. 222-62; Keith, *Buddhist Philosophy*, pp. 13-22; Mrs. Rhys Davids, *Sakya*, pp. 348-63.

It is possible that some portions of them were reduced to writing about the time of Asoka. The Rock Edicts of Asoka are evidence for the existence, in his day, of portions of Pitakas resembling those we now possess, but, indeed, no one disputes the existence of Oral Pitakas then. These Edicts, however, do not prove the existence of written Pitakas but only of an Oral tradition. We are still in the region of probabilities, and not of certainties so far as the question of *written* Pitakas is concerned. What is certain is that our *Pali Pitakas* were not in existence in the Asokan age, because the language, as we have it in all our books, was not then perfected.

Keith thinks that we have moderately secure grounds for thinking that in the two centuries after Asoka the Sutta-Pitakas of the Pali Canon was coming into being, and in the same period we may place the redaction of the Vinaya-Pitaka, in the composite form in which we now have it. The Abhidhamma probably was not completed until the second century A.D. or even later. In all the Pitakas there are elements of very early teaching mixed up with matter which is clearly later by centuries.[1]

Our difficulty is to separate the *primitive* teaching from the later additions, and what is most urgently needed is that the text of the Pali Pitakas should be investigated by experts, with the same conscientious care and critical minuteness, as has been applied to the Greek text of the New Testament. In no other way can we discover what the Buddha really believed and taught, for, at present, we can only guess at the truth.

Nevertheless, though such textual criticism of the *Canon*

[1] For more detailed information see the following Authorities: (1) Keith, *Buddhist Philosophy*, pp. 13-32; (2) Mrs. Rhys Davids, *Points of Controversy*, pp. xxix-xxxi; (3) Rhys Davids, *S.B.B.*, Vol. II, pp. xi ff.; (4) Rhys Davids, *S.B.E.*, Vol. XXXV, pp. xxvii ff.; (5) Rhys Davids, *Buddhist India*, pp. 161-87; (6) Mrs. Rhys Davids, *A Manual of Buddhism*, Chaps. I, II, and XIV; (7) Mrs. Rhys Davids, *Sakya*, Chaps. XIX, XXI, and Appendices I and V; (8) G. K. Nariman, *Sanskrit Buddhism*, Appendix I by Sylvain Levi.

by experts is essential for a proper understanding of Buddhism, orthodox Buddhists cannot tolerate even the suggestion of such an investigation. They accept all the Pitakas, even the Abhidhamma Pitaka (notwithstanding Buddhaghosa's testimony to the contrary, see *Points of Controversy*, p. xxx) as the original teaching of the Buddha. This is true, not only of the unlearned, but of Buddhist scholars as well. *Knowledge* must not interfere with *faith*.

The large place occupied by faith in Buddhism, however, is generally overlooked, both by Buddhists themselves, and by others.[1] But what we have said is confirmed by the confession of Shwe Zan Aung, B.A., a Buddhist scholar, who is an acknowledged authority upon the Pali Texts. He says :

' Personally, let me add, I am acting only as the mouth-piece of my country's teachers. I have no theories of my own. At best I am but an interpreter of Burmese views based on the Ceylon Commentary and the works of Budd-haghosa. You may take my essay as medieval Buddhism presented through modern Burmese glasses. And you may consider that the Burmese view, with the sole exception of Ledi Sadaw is, as a rule, one with Sumangala (i.e. Ceylon Cy.) and Buddhaghosa. Buddhists accept on faith the teaching that has been handed down from century to century. Now, in matters passing the possibility of verification, the nearest approach to proof is *to show the likelihood* of anything.'[2]

To sum up the evidence for the genuineness and reliability of the Buddhist *Pali* Canon, we may say that there is a strong presumption that the Pitakas contain teachings actually given by the Buddha, and, possibly, some of them

[1] On ' Faith ' in Buddhism, see Keith, pp. 33 and 34, and *S.B.B.*, Vol. III, pp. 99-100. (See also p. 52 of this book.)
[2] *Compendium of Philosophy*, being a translation of the *Abhidammattha-Sangaha*, P.T.S., pp. 283-84.

in the very form in which they were originally given, though not in the Buddha's own words, for we may be sure that he spoke to the people in their own vernaculars.

Now most of his work was carried on in the kingdoms of Kosala and Magadha. Therefore, we may safely assume that he habitually used the *Kosalan* and *Magadhan* dialects.

But *the words of the Buddha* have come down to us in Pali, and in a perfected form of Pali which, probably, had not even come into existence at the time when the Asokan inscriptions were made. Hence *the words of the Buddha* in the Pali Texts are translations into another language of the words and expressions he actually used. (See p. 15.)

Moreover, the fact that these teachings were not committed to writing until centuries after the death of the Teacher, but existed only in the form of an Oral tradition, makes it very difficult to decide what the original teachings were. Much has been written about the retentiveness and reliability of the trained Eastern memory, and, indeed, it was a wonderful instrument. The Brahman teacher taught his young disciple the *Vedas* word by word, sentence by sentence, and section by section, until he became *word-perfect*, and was able to repeat a whole book without hesitation or mistake. The disciple in turn, when he became master, taught his pupil in the same careful way, and so the *Vedas* were handed down intact from generation to generation. But, as Mrs. Rhys Davids points out,[1] there is no mention in the Pitakas of such *repeaters*. The nearest to it is the direction by the Buddha at the end of a discourse, ' Learn what has been said ; master it, bear it in mind.'[2]

The disciple would remember the substance of the sermons and talks of the Buddha, and some striking expressions would stick in the memory for life. So some modern sermon-lovers are able to relate, with remarkable accuracy, sermons they have heard, but they cannot give a

[1] *Sakya*, pp. 360, 384, and 389. [2] *Majjhima*, III, 199.

verbatim report, though a sentence here and there may be given in the very words of the preacher. Oft-repeated doctrines and formulas might be remembered in the words of the Master, but, for the rest, only the substance of the sayings, the ideas, would be retained, and each disciple would reproduce them in the best words at his command.

We have the testimony of the books themselves, and of Buddhist historians, to the fact that the Oral tradition became quickly corrupted, and that Councils had to be called from time to time, to decide what, indeed, was the *primitive* tradition. The splitting up of Buddhists into many contending sects is evidence of the same kind. Even in connexion with the Council of Rajagaha, we find recorded the incident of the monk Purana, who refused to accept the text adopted by the members of the Council, preferring his own recollection of the Buddha's words.[1] This must have been typical of individual Buddhists, and of Buddhist groups, throughout the early centuries. The Pali Texts themselves bear indisputable evidence of slow growth. No Buddhist scholar, unless restrained by faith from expressing an opinion, will deny the truth of this.

We must not give more space in this small book to the discussion of the Buddhist *Canon*, not because the subject is unimportant—it is of the greatest importance—but because discussions of the subject by experts are within the reach of most readers, and also because it is the writer's purpose to give most space to the discussion of those subjects which the young student, or ordinary reader, could not easily find in books on Buddhism.[2]

[1] See Geden's *Studies* note on page 223.
[2] See *A History of Pāli Literature*, by B. C. Law, Ph.D., M.A., B.L. (Kegan Paul, published 1933) for further information, especially the Introduction dealing with ' The Origin and Home of Pali,' and Chapter I, ' Chronology of The Pali Canon.' This valuable book came to hand when my MS. was ready for Press, therefore I was not able to consult it. But I recommend it to all students.

II

THE BUDDHA

WE DO NOT possess a contemporary biography of Gotama Buddha. We may even go farther and say that such an ancient biography never existed. For if it had, the fact must have been known to those who handed on the *Oral* tradition from the days of the Buddha to the time when the Pitakas were first reduced to writing. But the *Pali texts* neither contain a biography of the Buddha, nor the slightest reference to one having existed at any time. This evidence is conclusive.[1]

In ancient times, the disciples of great teachers concentrated rather upon the teaching than upon the lives of their masters. Any biographical details that they give us are, primarily, intended to form a framework for the teaching, and not to give us information about the teacher. The Christian Gospels frequently mention the day or hour, and the place, in which certain words were spoken, and certain deeds done by Jesus. But no attempt is made to give us a chronological series of events. We find, for example, such expressions as these : ' And He came down to Capernaum, a city of Galilee. And He was teaching them on the Sabbath day,' or ' And it came to pass on one of the days, as He was teaching the people in the temple.'

[1] It is true that the Mahayana Buddhists have a complete and detailed life of the Buddha, called the *Lalita Vistara*, but it is a poem of unknown date and authorship. It appears to have been composed by a Buddhist poet in Nepal, probably not less than 600, and possibly a 1000 years after the death of the Buddha, though some scholars believe it to be a composite work which took centuries to complete. It has no more value, as a source of information about the Buddha's life, than a medieval poem would have for the life of Christ. (See *The Hibbert Lectures*, 1881, by Rhys Davids, pp. 197-204, and *Sanskrit Buddhism*, by Nariman, p. 27.)

The Pitakas are even more vague. The Buddha's sermons and dialogues are usually introduced by such phrases as these : ' When the Exalted One was once journeying through Kosala,' or, ' The Exalted One was once staying at Savatthi,' or again, ' The Blessed One was once going along the high road between Rajagaha and Nalanda.' Then follows the statement that he spoke certain words, or met certain people.

In the absence of authentic biographies, we are thrown back upon the Pitakas, supplemented by certain other early books and traditions, for our information about the life of this great Teacher. The details seem discouragingly meagre, but close study of *the sources* reveals much information that was not apparent on the surface.

Attempts have been made by certain scholars to prove that Gotama was a purely mythical figure, who never had an historical existence. But we need not linger over these theories, because they are so contrary to both history and reason, that one would need to be abnormally credulous to accept them. This Teacher not only actually lived and taught, but, by his life and teachings, profoundly influenced all succeeding generations, and today millions of our race are proud to call him ' Master.'

Though there has been much dispute about the date of the Buddha's birth—dates differing by centuries having been suggested—it is now generally agreed amongst Western scholars that he died in 483 B.C., or very near that time, and as there is no reason to dispute the ancient tradition that he lived to his eightieth year, we may, with considerable confidence, accept 563 B.C. as the probable date of his birth.[1]

Gotama was a Sakya. The Sakya clan formed one of those small and aristocratic republics, which still survived in North India alongside the four important kingdoms

[1] See special note in *Sakya*, p. 434.

of Magadha, Kosala, Vamsas, and Avanti. Now, although the Sakyas were a small people, and were tributary to the King of Kosala, they were noted for their pride of race, and arrogance toward others. This is referred to in the Pitakas again and again, and many stories are told to illustrate it, but one will suffice.

It is said that Pasenadi, the King of Kosala, asked for one of the daughters of the Sakya chiefs as his wife. The chiefs were very indignant at this request, because they considered the royal family of Kosala inferior in birth to themselves. ' So they sent him a girl named Vasavha Khattiya, the daughter by a slave girl of one of their leading chiefs.' It is related that when the King at last discovered the trick that had been played upon him, he was so infuriated that he invaded the Sakya kingdom, took their city, and put to death many members of their clan. Whether the story is actually true or not, it illustrates the Sakyas' reputation for pride.[1]

[1] See *Buddhist India*, Rhys Davids, pp. 1-4.

III

THE BIRTH AND EARLY LIFE OF GOTAMA BUDDHA

THE MORE closely we inquire into the life of this great Teacher, the more we are impressed with the scantiness of the material preserved for us in the Pitakas. What they have preserved are memories, and impressions, and reminiscences of the Master, such as we ourselves have treasured up of the great men we have known—especially of those with whom we have been closely associated for years.

And, after all, the slight sketch of a great man contained in the brief and fragmentary *memoirs* of a personal friend will often bring him before us more vividly, and make us know him better, than the full and detailed portrait contained in a large official biography. Therefore, we need not be too greatly discouraged in our present inquiry, for a careful study of the materials at our disposal may give us richer results than we might have been disposed to believe possible.

But we have to face the fact, which we have already noticed (see pp. 18–19) that the earliest of the *Pitakas* was not reduced to writing until centuries after the Buddha's death, and that the primitive tradition had become so mixed up with apocryphal stories of a late date that it is very difficult to separate the true from the false. Nevertheless, amidst the mass of legendary stories, there are some that, by their simplicity and definiteness, impress one as being likely to be historically true, and it seems possible to trace, in outline at least, the early life of Gotama Buddha.

Our present purpose is to glean from the records such references to his early life as can be regarded, with some degree of confidence, as historically true, and then to draw from those incidents such inferences as they will legitimately bear. Because, if it be true that ' the child is father to the man,' we may find that the light cast by the childhood of this teacher, will illuminate much that is dark and mysterious in his later life.

Gotama was the son of Suddhodana, Raja, or Chieftain, of the Sakyas—a branch of the Kshatriya or warrior caste—who dwelt in a little kingdom, which was situated in the north-east part of what is now the United Provinces, and in the neighbouring district of Southern Nepal. This kingdom probably covered an area of about 900 square miles, and lay partly on the lower slopes of the Himalayas, and partly in the rich rice-bearing plain below. Its chief town was Kapilavatthu (or Kapilavastu) on the banks of the River Rohini, and 130 miles due north of the city of Benares.

Though the Sakyas belonged to the warrior caste, they were, at this time, an agricultural people, and lived chiefly by cultivating the fertile fields that lay within their territory, and by the raising of cattle.

Suddhodana was married to two daughters of a chief of the Koliyans, a neighbouring people. For many years after the marriage, both these wives remained childless, and this was a real grief and misfortune to the Raja. Proportionately great was his joy, therefore, when one day his chief wife, the Lady Maya, who was now in her forty-fifth year, told him that she was going to have a child. He immediately jumped to the conclusion that it would be a boy, and the Brahmans confirmed him in his belief.

As the time drew near, the Lady Maya asked Suddhodana's permission to go to her parents' house for her confinement; but, on the way there, while resting in the beautiful Lumbini Grove under the blossom-covered Sal trees, her son, the future Buddha, was born. As quickly and as carefully as possible the mother and child were carried back to Suddhodana's house, and there, seven days afterwards, the Lady Maya died. The child, however, found a loving and careful nurse in his mother's sister, the Lady Pajapati, his father's other wife.

On his name-giving day (i.e. when he was five days old) they gave him the name Siddhattha, which means ' He who has accomplished his aim.' His family name was Gotama, and by this name he was known in later life. The following legend is undoubtedly very ancient, and is probably founded on fact. An old ascetic, called Asita, a friend of Suddhodana, came to see the child, and foretold that he would become a Buddha. It is also said that on his name-giving day, certain Brahmans declared that he would become either a ' Universal Monarch ' or a Buddha.

Suddhodana became greatly alarmed at this prophecy that his son would become a Buddha, and anxiously asked the Brahmans, ' What shall my son see to make him retire from the world ? '

' The four signs.'

' What four ? '

' A decrepit old man, a diseased man, a dead man, and a monk.'

Then said the King, ' From this time forth, let no such persons be allowed to come near my son. It will never do for my son to become a Buddha.'

The legends tell us that, henceforth, Suddhodana surrounded his son with young folk, and men in the very prime of life ; the aged, the sick and diseased, the yellow-robed ascetics, were forbidden to come into his presence. He was to be kept in complete ignorance of the existence of sickness, disease, old age, and death. Even dead birds and animals were to be removed from the parks and gardens in the early morning before he was abroad, lest he should see them and begin to ask questions. These legends are so persistent, and all Buddhists are so fully agreed that it was the appearance of the ' four dreaded omens ' that drove Siddhattha from ' home ' to ' homelessness,' that there is probably some historical truth at the back of them.

It is probable that he married at an early age according to the custom of the country. He is said to have married his cousin, the daughter of the Raja of Koli. She is generally called ' the mother of Rahula,' but sometimes by the name Yasodhara.

This is practically all that we know of Gotama's early life, until we come to the events leading up to the ' Great Renunciation,' when he was about twenty-nine years old, and the consideration of these must be reserved for a later chapter.

IV

THE 'HOME LEAVING' OF GOTAMA
BUDDHA

As we think about Gotama Buddha and the work he
did in the world, the question arises in our minds : ' But
why did he leave home and go forth to the *homeless* life ? '
If we can find a satisfactory answer to that question, the
answers to many other questions, which are bound to arise
in the course of our inquiry, will not be so difficult to find.

Gotama's growing dissatisfaction with life may be
traced to his naturally pessimistic disposition, which had
been nourished and developed by his peculiar environment and training. Moreover, we have seen that in the
oldest records of his life—the *Pitakas*—history and legend
are so closely interwoven that it is no easy task to separate
the reliable strands of historical truth from the comparatively
worthless tangle of legendary stories.

Nevertheless, some of the recorded incidents in the
Buddha's life are so natural, and so characteristic of the
man as we now conceive him, as to make us feel that, if
they are not really historically true, they are true in spirit
(' true to life,' as we say) and contribute to our knowledge
of the real Buddha.

One such incident is recorded in the story of ' The
Four Visions.' We are told that the young prince, Siddhattha, became so restive under the conditions of restraint
and seclusion, in which his father had compelled him to
live, that he rebelled at last, and insisted on being allowed
to see for himself the life of the larger world outside the
walls of the royal parks and gardens.

Though Suddhodana dreaded the influence upon his son of contact with the common life of men, he could no longer restrain him, but he did the best he could under the circumstances, and ordered that the city should be so carefully prepared for his son's reception that no unpleasant sight or sound might distress him, and deepen the gloom of his heart. The whole city was to be bright and gay; the poor, the miserable, the diseased, were to be kept out of sight; no old person was to mingle with the crowds, and no corpse was to be carried through the streets of the city, while Siddhattha remained in it.

Nevertheless, in spite of all these precautions, the prince saw in succession the 'Four Dreaded Omens'; an old grey-headed toothless man, a man foul with disease, an uncovered corpse being carried to the burial-ground, and a yellow-robed ascetic with a calm and peaceful face.

This story is found in many forms. In some a deity appears to the prince under these various aspects; in others he sees real men; and one of the oldest authorities even speaks of ideas and not of visions; but the underlying teaching is the same in all. In the mind of Gotama there had grown up a horror of life—not only life as he knew it, but life under every conceivable condition. The thought that he himself, and those whom he loved, must inevitably grow old and die was intolerable to him. He was filled with fear as he thought of the possibility of becoming the victim of wasting sickness and disease. Life beyond the grave held out no hope for him, because he saw there only the same gloomy round of rebirth, sickness, old age, death, and ever-recurring rebirths and deaths. Surely life was the greatest evil, but might there not be some way of escape from life? The very thought of the possibility of such a way of escape enchanted him. He remembered the peaceful look on the ascetic's face, and thought that perhaps such a way of escape could be found in the *homeless* life. He resolved to put it to the test, and, as soon as possible, to surrender home and go forth into homelessness.

The deciding cause of his fleeing from home was the birth of his first and only son when he had been married for at least ten years. The news was brought to him as he sat in a garden by the river side. All the clansmen were rejoicing at the birth of this child—the Raja's only grandson, and a future heir to the throne—but the news brought no joy to the father's heart. He gave his son the name Rahula, meaning 'a fetter,' for he said, 'This is a new and strong tie I shall have to break.' He felt that, if he did not escape quickly, the tiny hands of his little son would hold him so firmly that he would never be able to break away, and he resolved to go that very night.

When the prince returned to the city he was received with congratulations and rejoicing. A young and beautiful princess, called Kisagotami, looked out of her window, and seeing the prince, exclaimed, 'Happy the father, happy the mother, happy the wife of such a son and husband!' Gotama heard her words, and said to himself, 'But whence comes the repose that brings happiness to the heart?'

The word 'happy' has a second, a religious, meaning —'freedom from transmigration'—and Gotama chose to understand and use it in that sense. He was grateful to the young girl for suggesting this thought to him, and removing his pearl necklace, he sent it to her, with the words, 'Let this be her fee as a teacher.' Kisagotami received it joyfully, saying, 'The prince is in love with me and will make me his second wife.' But the prince had other thoughts, and had already dismissed her from his mind.

It is recorded that, when he reached home, he found that his father had gathered together the most beautiful dancers in the country to cheer him, and to divert his mind from gloomy thoughts. Though they exercised every allurement to captivate his attention, in sheer weariness and boredom he fell asleep. When he awoke he saw all these beautiful girls lying asleep on the floor in various attitudes. He looked round upon them, and to his distorted mind, they appeared like disfigured corpses in a burial-place, and the house seemed to be full of flames. He cried out in his fear and pain, ' Alas! danger surrounds me. Alas! distress surrounds me. Now is the time come for me to go on the great pilgrimage.'

The thought of his little son intrudes into the midst of these other thoughts, and he feels impelled to look upon him just once before he forsakes him. Creeping quietly up to his wife's chamber, he finds her lying on the couch with her hand covering the child's head. Dearly would he have liked to take the baby into his arms, but dare not risk waking his wife, so he had to be content with a look, and then went silently away. We are glad to have this glimpse of the real human nature of Gotama : it is like a ray of sunlight in a dark cave.

Channa, Gotama's faithful servant, was waiting outside with his favourite horse, the snowy white Kanthaka, already saddled, and very quietly they stole out of the city. They travelled far that night—as far as the banks of a river called the Anoma, beyond the Koliyan territory. There he removed his jewels and ornaments, gave them to Channa, and told him to take them and the horse back to his father. Then Gotama cut off his long hair, exchanged clothes with a beggar, and, at the age of twenty-nine, began the homeless life as a wandering mendicant.

His action in leaving home for homelessness was not unique ; thousands of other Indians had done and were doing the same. This was especially true of the noble and cultured, i.e. those who had been able to experience for themselves all that the worldly life offered of power and pleasure. Just as, in later days, those who forsook the world to become disciples of the Buddha were chiefly 'the sons of noble houses,' so it had ever been ; men who had drunk deeply of the world's pleasures, like Prince Siddhattha, and had become satiated and filled with loathing, sought relief and satisfaction in the 'Religious Life,' and especially in a life of *homelessness* and asceticism.

The horror of life had so obsessed the mind of the young prince that his love for wife and child and aged father, and his duty to his people, had become of little account if only he could find a way of escape from his torment. His experience was similar to that of Bunyan's immortal 'Pilgrim,' and is well known in the sphere of religion. His mind was entirely occupied with one fact, that all life is sorrow, and all his mental and moral powers were concentrated on one point: how to save himself from sorrow.

As a devout Buddhist has said :

'Gotama does not begin his career as a Saviour of the world. Nothing lies farther from his mind than the welfare of others. He seeks his own salvation, and that only. It is a purely egotistical impulse, but what more natural than that one who suddenly finds himself in a burning house should seek first of all to save himself ? However, after he has attained this salvation, his mind turns back to his suffering fellow-men, and only now in the retrospective motion do we see love emerge in the shape of the compassion that comprehends. He himself characteristically says : "There are two reasons why I follow this manner of life, my own well-being in this present life, and sympathy with those that follow me." '[1]

The tradition that Gotama, on the morning after he left home, cut off his hair, and exchanged his princely robes for the rags and begging bowl of a mendicant, may be accepted with some confidence, and the *authorities* are unanimous that he first of all made his way to Rajagaha, the capital of Magadha, and the seat of the powerful King

[1] Paul Dahlke, *Buddhist Essays*, pp. 130-31.

Bimbisara. Here he went through the streets of the city, begging-bowl in hand, begging his food from door to door, like any other religious mendicant.

The story that the mixed mess of food he had collected filled him with loathing, so that at first he could not bring himself to eat it, has the ring of truth. However, the reflection that he was now a homeless mendicant, and that henceforth such food would be his daily fare, enabled him to overcome his natural revulsion once for all.

It is related, further, that the news that Prince Siddhattha had become a religious mendicant spread far and wide, and that the common people gave him not only the respect due to a mendicant, but also the honour due to the son of a reigning chief. Even King Bimbisara is said to have offered him a suitable home in Rajagaha with daily provision, but the young mendicant courteously refused the offer : he could not settle anywhere, or find rest, until he had solved the enigma of life and brought rebirth to an end.

First of all, he sought help from the great religious teachers of his day, and became the disciple of Alara of Kalama, one of the most renowned of them all, and learnt everything that he had to teach him of religion and philosophy. But when, at last, Alara confessed that he did not know how to bring rebirth to an end, Gotama left him. After that he sat at the feet of Uddaka, another famous teacher, who taught him much, but could not give him the special knowledge which he sought, so he left him also and went on his sorrowful way.

Having abandoned all hope of obtaining this knowledge from teachers, he resolved to become an ascetic, and, if possible, to attain his end through self-torture. With this purpose in his heart he withdrew into the jungle of Uruvela, near the present temple of Buddha-gaya, and there, along with five other ascetics, he underwent the most incredible bodily and mental sufferings. As he went far beyond the other ascetics in self-torture they acknowledged him as their chief. But his greatest distress was caused by the growing conviction that all his sufferings were bringing him no nearer to his goal.

After six years of this torment, being almost in despair, he made a supreme effort and fell down as one dead. In fact, his disciples thought he was dead, and exclaimed: ' Gotama the Sakya has died without attaining his object.'

He was not dead, however, for after a little while, he recovered consciousness and took food. Then the ascetics abandoned him and went to Benares, because he seemed to them to have utterly failed.

He was very weary and depressed, and was hurt by the desertion of his disciples, so he went and sat under the shade of a great Bo-tree and began to take stock of his life, ' For,' said he, ' I have left all that men count dear in order to attain to this knowledge, and I have suffered all that man can suffer, and yet I seem no nearer the goal of my desire. Would it not be wiser for me now to give up this fruitless search, and to return to my country and people where I am sure of a great welcome?' The temptation was very strong, but he resisted it, and determined to continue his search for release even though death overtook him on the way.

It was clear that there was no more to be hoped for from asceticism than from his former teachers, and he determined to practise it no more, but in future to eat sufficient food to keep his body and mind in the highest state of efficiency. The outcome of his meditation was a resolve to remain seated under the Bo-tree until he found either the way of escape from sorrow, or death. He did not seek, or expect, help from any god or man, but relied upon his own unaided efforts for success. And we are told that, after resisting all the temptations of *Mara* and utterly defeating him, he finally attained to that knowledge, that enlightenment and illumination, which made him the Buddha.

And what was this supreme knowledge that came to Gotama while he meditated under the Bo-tree ? It was the knowledge of the universal law of cause and effect : the knowledge that at the back of phenomenal existence there is no personal, intelligent Creator and Ruler of the universe, but only impersonal, mechanical law—*the law of becoming and passing away*. As Buddhaghosa says : ' The wheel of Becoming is without known beginning, lacking both Maker, such as Brahma, and precipient " I ". For each consequent proceeds by reason of its antecedent.'[1]

In a word, this great discovery, which was to revolutionize all human thought and life, was that there is in the universe neither substance nor spirit—neither underlying reality in matter, nor God nor soul at the back of mind—but only the law of becoming and passing away ; the law of impermanence which inevitably involves evil and sorrow.

This discovery brought great peace and satisfaction to the heart of Gotama, because he perceived in it a way of escape from sorrow and rebirth. For it is evident that, if there is no *real* soul to be reborn rebirth *can* be brought to an end.

While he was thus meditating on the fruits of victory, two merchants (at the instigation of a deity) offered food in an alms-bowl (provided by the gods) to the Buddha, who accepted it at their hands, and was refreshed and strengthened after his long fast. Then these merchants asked to be accepted as his adherents and they became his first lay-followers. After that the Buddha sat for a long time under the Bo-tree enjoying the peace and rest that had come to him after the toil and strife. The thought, ' This is my last life; I shall never more be reborn,' was ineffable bliss to him.

At length, however, his mind wandered from himself to the needs of gods, and men, and other living beings : could anything be done to help them ? would it be worth while to make known his great discovery to them ? could

[1] See Mrs. Rhys Davids, *Buddhism*, pp. 97-99.

they possibly appreciate this great doctrine that had cost him so much ? And as he reflected upon the ignorance, the stupidity, and the low mentality of men, he was strongly tempted to keep his gospel to himself and not to preach it to the world. He said, ' Should I now preach the Doctrine and mankind not understand me, it would bring me nothing but fatigue, it would cause me nothing but trouble ! ' And there passed unceasingly through the mind of the Exalted One this voice, which no one had ever heard before :

> Why reveal to the world what I have won by a severe struggle?
> The truth remains hidden from him whom desire and hate absorb.
> It is difficult, mysterious, deep, hidden from the coarse mind ;
> He cannot comprehend it, whose mind earthly vocations surround with night.

When Brahma Sahampati perceived the state of the Buddha's mind, he became alarmed for the future welfare of gods and men, and, descending from heaven, pleaded their cause with the Buddha. The compassionate pleading of Brahma overcame the doubts and fears of the Buddha, and he agreed to give living beings a chance to hear and receive his Doctrine. And he said to Brahma Sahampati these words :

> Let opened be to all the door of eternity ;
> He who hath ears, let him hear the word and believe.
> I thought of affliction for myself, therefore have I, O Brahma,
> Not yet proclaimed the noble word to the world.

Now the Buddha had overcome every obstacle, and had become not only a Buddha, but the Universal Buddha, the Exalted One far above gods and men.[1]

---

[1] See Oldenberg's *Buddha*, pp. 121-23.

The Buddha was exercised in his mind as to who was most worthy to hear his Doctrine first. His mind turned to his two teachers, and he resolved to preach it to them, but found that they were both dead. Then he thought of the five ascetics, his former companions, and he decided to preach to them. He found them in the Deer Park, Isipatana, at Benares. They received him courteously but coldly, and addressed him simply by his name, and called him ' Friend.' But the Buddha rebuked them sharply, saying, ' Ye monks, address not the Perfect One (Tathagata) by his name, and call him not " Friend ". The Perfect One, O Monks, is the holy supreme Buddha. Open ye your ears O monks, the deliverer from death is found : I teach you, I preach the Law.' The ascetics raised further objections, but the Buddha overwhelmed them by his dignity and authority, so that they were convinced, and submitted to be taught by him.

Then he preached to them his first sermon about the ' Middle Way ' and the ' Sacred Truth of Suffering.' This was the famous sermon at Benares, with which the Buddha opened his ministry, set rolling *the Wheel of the Law*. This Sermon was typical of all his sermons, for he had only one subject : suffering and the deliverance from suffering. The five ascetics accepted this fundamental doctrine, and were received into the Order. ' At this time,' so ends the narrative, ' there were six holy persons in the world '—the Buddha himself, and these five disciples.[1]

Gotama's next convert was a young man called Yasa. The history of this man is so much like that of Prince Siddhattha, that some authorities suggest that the story of the convert has, through an error, been applied to the Master.

[1] For a full description and discussion of the Sermon at Benares, see Oldenberg's *Buddha*, pp. 125-31.

Yasa was the son of wealthy, and influential, people living in Benares. He had been brought up in the greatest luxury, and his every desire and passion had been indulged. Though still quite young, he had a large harem of beautiful women. But the closest parallel of Yasa's story to that of Siddhattha is seen in the fact that, in his case, as in Siddhattha's, it was the sight of the beautiful women lying asleep that created in Yasa's heart a deep disgust for the life of sensual indulgence, and a firm resolve to escape from that manner of life at all costs.

Crying aloud, ' Alas ! What sorrow ! What danger ! ' he fled from the house in terror and despair, and coming into the presence of the Buddha craved his help. The Buddha, seeing that Yasa's experience of life had fully prepared him to receive his fundamental doctrine of suffering and the way of escape from suffering, taught him this doctrine without any reservations, and Yasa accepted it with joy, and became a disciple.

Many other sons of wealthy, and noble houses—Yasa's friends—began to join the Buddha's company, and soon his adherents numbered sixty.

The Buddha now sent forth these sixty disciples in all directions to spread the good news that a way of escape from misery had been found, and that rebirth could be brought to an end. But he himself returned to Uruvela, where dwelt a thousand ascetics, under the leadership of the Brahman, Kassapa, and his two brothers. Kassapa, we are told, had given up a great position, and wealth, and a beautiful wife, to become an ascetic.

The Buddha took up his abode near the dwelling-place of these ascetics, and took his food with them every day, and performed wonderful miracles which filled them with admiration, and did everything in his power to win them as disciples. The story is too long to be related in detail here. Suffice to say that Kassapa their leader, was the first of the ascetics to submit to the Buddha, and acknowledge him as Master. Kassapa's two brothers, however, and the rest of the ascetics, as might have been expected, quickly followed his example, so that the Buddha gained a thousand disciples at Uruvela.

The Buddha now proceeded with his large band of followers to Rajagaha, the capital of Magadha, where the king, Bimbisara, with a great multitude of Brahmans and citizens, went forth to meet him. Bimbisara and many of the citizens declared themselves lay-followers of the Buddha. Here, too, the Buddha won over two Brahmans, Sariputta and Moggallana, who eventually became, perhaps, the greatest of his disciples.

We are told, further, that many noble youths, from the best families in Magadha, came to the Buddha and cast in their lot with him. This produced dismay and anger amongst the people ; so much so, indeed, that they cried out in their indignation, ' The ascetic Gotama is come to bring subversion of families.' They felt that the best of their young men would be drawn away from their family, their social, and their national duties and responsibilities to seek their own good, instead of the good of the community.

The Buddha, however, shared the views of that ancient Brahman, who said : ' The intelligent and wise desire not posterity ; what are descendants to us, whose home is the *Atman ?* They relinquish the desire for children, the struggle for wealth, the pursuit of worldly weal, and go forth as mendicants.' Therefore, the Buddha went calmly on his way making disciples, and the excitement soon died down.

We read that, about this time, Gotama, at the earnest request of his father, agreed to pay a visit to Kapilavatthu, and great was the joy of the Raja and his people, and great were the preparations made for his reception, when they heard the glad news that their prince was returning to them

again. The Buddha, however, stole quietly into the city,
and, to the distress and indignation of his father, was discovered begging his food from door to door like any
ordinary mendicant. Nevertheless, the Buddha is represented as so far overcoming the objections of his father,
Suddhodana, and his wife, Yasodhara, to his manner of
life, that the former became a lay-adherent, and the latter
allowed her son, Rahula, to have his head shaved, and to
join the mendicant band of his father, the Buddha. Moreover, three of the Sakya princes, Ananda, Anuruddha, and
Devadatta, his cousins, entered the Order, together with
Upali, a barber, who afterwards became a great disciple.

The Buddha now returned to Rajagaha where the rich
merchant, Anathapindika, gave him the famous Jetavana
Park, at Savatthi, with its beautiful gardens, in which were
' residences for the brethren, houses, halls, storerooms, surrounded by lotus ponds, fragrant mango trees, shady
arcades, and leafy walks.' Here also was a ' fragrance
chamber ' for the Buddha's own use. King Bimbisara, too,
gave him his own pleasure garden called Veluvana (' Bambu-
grove '), and similar gifts were given by a rich lady named
Visakha, and, much later, by the courtesan, Ambapali ;
and there arose a keen rivalry between the chief towns
for the honour of housing Gotama and his monks.

Thus briefly have we sketched the early days of the
Buddha's career as a public teacher. We would draw special
attention to the enthusiastic reception of Gotama Buddha
by the civil and religious leaders of Kosala and Magadha,
where he spent his life in preaching and teaching.[1] We will
deal more particularly with the Buddha's popularity and
its causes in a later chapter.

[1] For more detailed information about the Public Work of Gotama
Buddha, see the following books: (1) Rhys Davids, *Buddhism*, pp. 53-69;
(2) Oldenberg, *Buddha: His Life, His Doctrine, His Order*, pp. 113-37; (3)
Sacred Books of the Buddhists, Vols. II-VI.

V

THE PUBLIC MINISTRY OF GOTAMA
BUDDHA

THE CONNECTED narrative of Gotama's Public Ministry
ends with the conversion of his two greatest disciples,
Sariputta and Moggallana, and it is not taken up again
until a period shortly before his death. Of the long intervening ministry of more than forty years we have only a
collection of undated—and undatable—incidents, discourses, and dialogues, with short notes of place and company as a background, but there is no information given
which would enable us to fix even an approximate date.

As we read the *Pitakas*, however, we are impressed by
the fact that the Buddha and his disciples lived their lives
according to strict rules—one year, for them, was very much
like every other year. They used to spend about nine
months of the year in wandering about the country, and the
remaining three months of *Vassa* (or *Was*), the rainy season,
in quiet retirement in the neighbourhood of towns and
villages where nobles and wealthy men contended with one
another for the honour of feeding them, and of providing
for their other needs.

The territory of the Buddha's wanderings was a comparatively small portion of *Aryan* India. It was called the
'Eastern Land' (in contrast to 'Western Hindustan,'
the ancient seat of *Vedic* culture, where the Brahmans were
all-powerful), and included the old kingdoms of Kosala
and Magadha, and the free States round about them—
the territories known today as Oudh and Bihar. He does
not appear to have influenced, to any great extent at least,

' Western Hindustan,' but his itinerary seems to have been between Savatthi (Sahet Mahet), the capital city of Kosala, on the north-west, and Rajagaha (Rajgar) the capital of Magadha, on the South-east. The distance between these two cities, as Oldenberg points out, was about the same as that between London and Edinburgh.

He spent the rainy season, as a rule, at one or other of these cities, where he had beautiful parks, and gardens, and dwelling-places for himself and his disciples, and lay followers to supply their needs. Moreover, it is probable that he did his most effective work in these great centres of population, and most of his recorded discourses are associated with either Rajagaha or Savatthi.

But though we cannot follow the Buddha's history month by month, and year by year, there has been preserved for us a very detailed account of his daily habits, which we may accept with considerable confidence.[1] Rising very early in the morning it was his daily habit, first of all, to accept water from his body-servant to rinse-out his mouth, and afterwards to sit down and meditate until it was time for him to go begging. Then, taking his alms-bowl in hand, he went out into the town or village, with eyes fixed on the ground, and passed silently from door to door, accepting whatever food was put into his bowl.

If he were invited to take his meal in a house, he usually accepted the invitation and ate whatever was put before him. The meal being over, he washed his hands, discoursed to those present on his doctrine, and then returned to the place where he was staying at the time. After sitting quietly on one side while his disciples finished their meal, he retired to his chamber and allowed his body-servant to bring him water to wash his feet. This being done, he returned again to the assembly of the disciples, and addressed them on some point of doctrine or discipline.

[1] See Warren, *Buddhism in Translations*, pp. 91-95.

The discourse ended, he retired again to his 'fragrance' chamber and rested through the heat of the day, and then, rising refreshed, he went out to receive visitors, and, after accepting their gifts, he taught them such doctrine as he considered suitable for them. When the visitors had gone away, he would go to bathe at the bath-house, or at some bathing-tank or pond, and would afterwards retire to his chamber for further meditation.

When the evening was come, it was his custom to receive any of his disciples who had come to see him from a distance, giving them counsel and advice, and clearing up any difficulties they might have, so that he sent them away cheered and strengthened. The evening being now far advanced, and feeling cramped with so much sitting, the Buddha would spend some time in just pacing up and down to relieve his legs until it was time for him to retire to his room for the night.

Though it must have been very difficult to observe these rules while on his journeys, he seems to have kept them as far as possible.

As we read the *Pitakas*, we are impressed with the popularity of the Buddha and his doctrine. Wherever he went, with a few exceptions, he was received with open arms by the nobles, and the common people usually followed their lead. If they were not willing to do this, it would appear that sometimes pressure was put upon them by the ruling families, for we read that, when the Buddha visited the town of Kusinara, 'the Mallas, the ruling family of the town, went out to meet him, and issued an edict, "Whosoever goeth not to meet the Exalted One is liable to a penalty of five hundred pieces." '

When he came to Vesali, probably the gayest and most dissolute town in India, the noble Licchavi youths drove out to meet him with their splendid teams, and so magnificent were they that the Buddha compared them to the divine host of the *thirty-three gods*. Ambapali, the famous courtesan of that town, drove out to meet him in no less splendour, and invited him and his disciples to dine with her at her mango grove. The Buddha accepted her invitation, and, when the meal was over, Ambapali presented the grove to the Buddha and his Order.[1]

Though the Brahmans are sometimes represented as being opposed to him, they were, according to the *Pitakas*, generally won over by his courtesy, tact, and dialectical skill. In fact, a great many Brahmans became his disciples.

But how are we to explain this almost universal popularity ?

(1) First of all, he belonged to the noble Sakya race, and was the eldest son of a ruling prince. Therefore, he met kings and nobles as an equal, and was accepted as one of themselves.

(2) He and his followers formed part of a great popular religious movement, the *Samana* movement. Religious mendicants were universally honoured ; so much so, indeed, that, if the king's slave went out from *home* to *homelessness* and donned the yellow-robe, the king himself was compelled, if not by personal conviction or inclination, by the popular sentiment of the people, to ' greet him with reverence, and rise from his seat in deference to him, and press him to be seated.'[2] Nothing could more fully illustrate the popularity of Religious Mendicancy than that. This applied not only to the Buddha's sect, but to all the other sects of *Samanas* as well.

(3) But there was another reason for respecting the Buddha and his Order, for not only the Buddha, but most of his disciples were ' sons of noble houses,' either Brahmans, or Kshatriyas, or sons of Merchant Princes. Therefore,

---

[1] For a full account of this visit see *S.B.B.*, Vol. III, pp. 102-5.
[2] *S.B.B.*, Vol. II, pp. 57 and 77.

apart altogether from religion, they would be well-received by the people.

(4) On the other hand, there was no organized religious opposition to the Buddha and his teaching. The picture of a united Brahmanism opposing the Buddha, as the Pharisees and Sadducees opposed Jesus, or as the Papacy opposed Luther, is unhistorical. Brahmanism, in the regions covered by the Buddha's ministry, was represented by a number of independent teachers, each with his own band of followers. These communities of *Samanas* were scarcely distinguishable from that of the Buddha. They were all celibates, wore the yellow-robe, and daily begged their food from house to house. Moreover there was a great body of teaching, and many practices, common to them all.[1] It was only in the region of higher doctrine that the radical differences between the Buddha's teaching and that of many of the other great teachers was apparent, as, for example, in their doctrines of the *summum bonum*, which the Buddha declared to be *Nirvana*, and the Brahmans *Oneness with Brahman*. But the Buddha never attempted to popularize his peculiar teachings ; he reserved them for the intelligent and devout few.

(5) It is also a mistake to represent the Buddha as a Radical Social Reformer. The statement that he maintained the right of men of all castes to enter the religious life is true, and men, suited in other respects to enter his Order, were not debarred by their caste.[2] But, long before Gotama was born, the ranks of the *Samanas* were open to the low-born as well as to the high-born, so that the Buddha was merely adopting a practice which had already become common in India. As a matter of actual fact, it is probable that the Buddha's Order contained a much higher percentage of high-caste men and women than many of the other contemporary Orders.

[1] See S.B.B., Vol. II, pp. 57–59. [2] See p. 112.

(6) Where he did oppose the Brahmans, as, for example, in discrediting their Sacrificial System, he did it in such a calm, unemotional, and impersonal way as to disarm resentment. There was nothing of the vehement reformer about him, none of the passion and zeal that arouses opposition and inevitably leads to persecution.

We are now in a position to answer the question why Gotama Buddha was so popular in India.

In almost every age and country a good man, who is prepared to live his own life, and not to interfere unduly with the lives and beliefs of other people, is not merely tolerated, but respected. Gotama Buddha was such a man. As we have already seen, his life and character, judged by the standards of his country and age, were above reproach, and he also demanded from his disciples the strictest moral conduct.

Moreover, though he was pre-eminent amongst contemporary religious teachers in India, and was, probably, the greatest man India has ever produced, he was still the child of his age and harmonized perfectly with his environment. Hence, his countrymen welcomed him, praised him, and were proud that he belonged to their race.

VI

THE LAST WORDS AND DEATH OF GOTAMA BUDDHA

NOTE.—In this chapter the passages within inverted commas are quotations from the *Mahaparinibbana Suttanta*.

The other passages are my own summary of the *Suttanta*, a short paragraph often condensing pages of the original.

C.H.S.W.

IN THE *Mahaparinibbana Suttanta*, or 'The book of the Great Decease,'[1] we have a detailed account of the closing months of the Buddha's life, and his last great journey from Rajagaha to Kusinara, where he died. This narrative is, probably, in the main trustworthy, though certain later material appears to have been introduced into the original narrative by the editors of the Pali Text with the idea of adding to the Buddha's glory.

The Buddha was eighty years old when he undertook this journey. For forty-four years he had been wandering about on foot from place to place, preaching his doctrine, and making disciples. In his later years he had seen much trouble. The revolt of his cousin, Devadatta, must have been a sore trial to him. Moreover, about a year before the Buddha's death, Ajatasattu, the parricide King of Magadha, invaded the kingdom of Kosala, and slew the king and the princes of the royal houses of Kosala and Kapilavatthu, the Buddha's kinsmen. In addition to these more personal troubles and losses, there was the ever increasing difficulty of maintaining discipline in the Order—there are many indications of this in the records.

[1] *Sacred Books of the Buddhists*, Vol. III, pp. 71ff.

The Buddha, worn out with labours and troubles, and knowing that his end was drawing near, turned his eyes to the north; he wished to die in sight of the snows of the Himalayas, amid the scenes of his youth.

He appears to have been in Rajagaha, the chief town of the Magadha kingdom, when he came to this decision, and he determined to journey northwards, by easy stages, speaking his last words of advice and warning to his disciples as they assembled to meet him in the chief centres of Buddhist influence on the way.

No useful purpose would be served by attempting to describe the Buddha's itinerary in detail. It is of the greatest interest and importance, however, to know what he considered to be the most vital things to be said to his followers in these last interviews. We will, therefore, in the following pages, give representative extracts from his speeches and conversations.

After bidding farewell to the *Sangha* in Rajagaha, with many words of advice as to their future conduct, he starts out on his journey and crosses the Ganges at Pataligama, where the new capital of Magadha was being built. This city was afterwards called Pataliputta (modern Patna), and became the chief town of India. The Suttanta describes this crossing as of a miraculous nature, as we read on pages 94 and 95, 'But the Exalted One went on to the river. And at that time the river Ganges was brimful and overflowing; and wishing to cross to the opposite bank, some began to seek for boats, some for rafts of wood, whilst some made rafts of basket-work. Then the Exalted One as instantaneously as a strong man would stretch forth his arm, or draw it back again when he had stretched it forth, vanished from this side of the river, and stood on the further bank with the company of the brethren.'

Leaving the river, 'The Exalted One proceeded with a great company of the brethren to Kotigama. And at that

place the Exalted One addressed the brethren, and said :
" It is through not understanding and grasping four Aryan
Truths, O brethren, that we have had to run so long, to
wander so long in this weary path of transmigration, both
you and I ! "

' " And what are these four ? "

' " The Aryan truth about sorrow ; the Aryan truth
about the cause of sorrow ; the Aryan truth about the
cessation of sorrow ; and the Aryan truth about the path
that leads to that cessation. But when these Aryan truths
are grasped and known the craving for future life is rooted
out, that which leads to renewed becoming is destroyed,
and then there is no more birth ! "

' Thus spake the Exalted One ; and when the Happy
One had thus spoken, then again the Teacher said : " By
not seeing the Aryan Truths as they really are, Long is
the path that is traversed through many a birth ;
When these are grasped, the cause of rebirth is removed,
The root of sorrow uprooted, and then there is no more
birth." '[1]

The Buddha was weary of answering the questions of
Ananda as to what had happened to this or that devout
man who had died. Therefore he determined to give him
an answer which would cover all cases. So, at Nadika, the
Exalted One spoke as follows :

' There is nothing strange in this, Ananda, that a human
being should die ; but that as each one does so you should
come to me, and inquire about them in this manner, that is
wearisome to me. I will, therefore, teach you a way of
truth, called the Mirror of Truth, which if a disciple of the
noble ones possess he may, if he should so desire, himself
predict of himself : " Purgatory is destroyed for me, and
rebirth as an animal, or a ghost, or in any place of woe. I
am converted, I am no longer liable to be reborn in a state

[1] *Sacred Books of the Buddhists*, Vol. III, pp. 96-97.

of suffering, and am assured of hereafter attaining to the enlightenment " (of *Arahantship*).

' What then, Ananda, is this Mirror of Truth ? It is the consciousness that the disciple of the *Arahants* is in this world possessed of faith in the Buddha.

' Is possessed of faith in the Truth—believing the Truth to have been proclaimed by the Exalted One, and to be attained to by the wise, *each one for himself*.

' Is possessed of faith in the Order—believing the multitude of the disciples of the Exalted One, who are walking in the four stages of the Noble Eightfold Path to be worthy of honour, of hospitality, of gifts and of reverence ; to be the supreme sowing-ground of merit for the world.'[1]

In the course of his journey the Buddha arrives at Vesali. In this city he had met with great success, and had many disciples.

Here the famous courtesan, Ambapali, came to see him, and invited him, together with his company, to take a meal at her house in her mango grove on the morrow. This invitation was accepted by the Buddha, to the great annoyance of the young nobles of Vesali, who came shortly afterwards with a similar invitation. At the close of the meal, ' Ambapali addressed the Exalted One, and said : " Lord, I present this pleasaunce to the order of mendicants, of which the Buddha is the Chief." And the Exalted One accepted the gift ; and after instructing, and rousing, and inciting, and gladdening her with religious discourse, he rose from his seat and departed thence.'[2]

From Vesali the Buddha went to Belúva, a village not far from the city. Here he directed his followers to distribute themselves among friends and acquaintances in and about Vesali for the retreat in the rainy season (*Vassa*), which was just upon them. But he himself remained at

---

[1] *Sacred Books of the Buddhists*, Vol. III, pp. 99-100.
[2] ibid., p. 105.

Beluva, with Ananda, to pass in solitude the last rainy season of his life.

Here a severe illness seized him, and he came nigh unto death. Ananda was in despair. But the Buddha, realizing that it would be a calamity to die there, before his work was finished, aroused himself, and by sheer force of will over-came the sickness, to the great joy of Ananda, who said, ' I took some comfort from the thought that the Exalted One would not pass away until at least he had left instruc-tions as touching the Order.'

' What, then, Ananda ? Does the Order expect that of me ? I have preached the truth without making any dis-tinction between *exoteric* and *esoteric* doctrine ; for in respect of the truth, Ananda, the Tathagata has no such thing as the closed fist of a teacher who keeps some things back. Surely, Ananda, should there be any one who har-bours the thought, " It is I who will lead the brotherhood," or, " The Order is dependent upon me," it is he who should lay down instructions in any matter concerning the Order.

' Now the Tathagata, Ananda, thinks not that it is he who should lead the brotherhood, or that the Order is dependent upon him. Why then should he leave instruc-tions in any matter concerning the Order ?

' Therefore, O Ananda, be ye lamps unto yourselves. Be ye a refuge to yourselves. Betake yourselves to no external refuge, holding fast to the Truth as a lamp, holding fast as a refuge to the Truth, looking not for refuge to any one besides himself ?

' And whosoever, Ananda, either now or after I am dead, shall be a lamp unto themselves, and a refuge unto them-selves, shall betake themselves to no external refuge, but holding fast to the Truth as their lamp, and holding fast as their refuge to the Truth, shall look not for refuge to any one besides themselves—it is they, Ananda, among

my bhikkhus, who shall reach the very topmost Height!—
but they must be anxious to learn.'[1]

Leaving Vesali the Buddha and his company go on to
Bhanda-gama. 'There the Exalted One addressed the
brethren, and said: "It is through not understanding and
grasping four truths (Not the Four Noble Truths of
Suffering mentioned above), O brethren, that we have had
to run so long, to wander so long in this weary path of
transmigration—both you and I.

'"And what are these four? The noble conduct of life,
the noble earnestness in meditation, the noble kind of
wisdom, and the noble salvation of freedom. When these
four are realized and known—then is the craving for future
life rooted out, that which leads to renewed existence is
destroyed, and there is no more birth." '[2]

From Bhanda-gama the Buddha went to Pava. 'And
there at Pava the Exalted One stayed at the mango grove
of Chunda, who was by family a smith' (p. 137). Chunda
invited the Buddha to a meal. Amongst the food set before
him, there was a dish of pork of which he partook freely,
and felt greatly strengthened. Shortly afterwards, however,
his old sickness, dysentery, came upon him with renewed
violence. He thanked Chunda for his hospitality, and then
quickly moved on lest Chunda should reproach himself
for the Buddha's illness.[3]

Sick and weary the Buddha pressed on toward Kusinara.
Arriving there at last they proceeded to the sala grove of the
Mallas, the Upavattana of Kusinara, on the farther side of
the River Hiranyavati. 'Then he said to Ananda: "Spread
over for me, I pray you, Ananda, the couch with its head
to the north, between the twin sala trees. I am weary,
Ananda, and would lie down!" And the Exalted One

[1] *Sacred Books of the Buddhists*, Vol. III, pp. 107-9.
[2] ibid., pp. 131-32.
[3] See pp. 56–57.

laid himself down on his right side, with one leg resting on the other; and he was mindful and self-possessed'; [1] and as he lay the Sala blossoms kept falling upon him.

Ananda was greatly troubled that he was about to lose his Master, and he turned aside weeping at the thought: ' Alas! I remain still but a learner, one who has yet to work out his own perfection. And the Master is about to pass away from me—he who is so kind.'

But the Buddha sent for him, and after commending him, in the presence of them all, for his faithful service, concluded his speech with these words: ' You have done well, Ananda! Be earnest in effort, and you too shall soon be free from the intoxications—(of sensuality, and individuality, and delusion, and ignorance).' ' That is to say, " You too shall become an Arahant." ' [2]

Then follows an account of the conversion of Subhadda, the Wanderer, who after a little intense meditation attained the supreme goal of the higher life (Nirvana).

' So the venerable Subhadda became yet another among the Arahants; and he was the last disciple whom the Exalted One himself converted.' [3]

The Buddha asked whether any from the 500 assembled brethren had any doubt or misgiving as to the Buddha, or the Doctrine, or the Path, or the Method. And if so, to inquire freely, so that they might not afterwards have to reproach themselves with the thought: ' Our Teacher was face to face with us, and we could not bring ourselves to inquire of the Exalted One when we were face to face with him.' But not any of the brethren had any question to ask. Then the Buddha revealed to them that not one out of that great company had any doubt or misgiving

---

[1] *Sacred Books of the Buddhists*, Vol. III, p. 149.
[2] ibid., pp. 157-59.
[3] ibid., p. 169.

in his mind, and that every one of them was assured of attaining to the *Enlightenment of Arahantship*.

'Then the Exalted One addressed the brethren, and said : " Behold now, brethren, I exhort you, saying : ' Decay is inherent in all component things ! Work out your salvation with diligence ! ' " This was the last word of the Tathagata.' [1]

Having said this, the Buddha passed into the first trance, and from that into the second, and so through the third and the fourth : and then back again through the third, and the second to the first, and from that he passed into *Parinirvana*.[2]

The funeral rites of the Buddha were performed by the nobles of Kusinara, and they burned his body with all the honours shown to the body of a universal monarch.[3]

Some modern scholars suggest that Gotama did not eat pork, but a kind of truffle of which pigs are very fond, hence the name. But there was no reason why he should not eat pork. He never prohibited the eating of flesh. For special reasons he prohibited the eating of certain kinds of flesh. For example, he forbade his bhikkhus to eat the flesh of elephants and horses, because they were royal animals, and belonged to the king. And again, they were not to eat the flesh of savage beasts, such as leopards and tigers, because the bhikkhu who did this could no longer walk safely in the forests.

Neither the bhikkhus nor the lay-Buddhists of Ceylon are vegetarians, as a rule. Some Buddhists will not eat beef, either for totemistic reasons, or under the influence of Hinduism. Many Sinhalese Buddhists are fishermen and hunters, and the slaughter of animals for food is not uncommon in Buddhist communities. No true Buddhist,

[1] *Sacred Books of the Buddhists*, Vol. III, pp. 172-73.
[2] ibid., pp. 174-75.
[3] See *Sakya*, pp. 339-47.

however, will eat an egg, though he may eat flesh and fish freely.

Sometimes appeals to Buddhists to refrain from eating flesh during such seasons as *Wesak* and *Poson* are published in the newspapers, and probably many Buddhists respond to these appeals. The following is an example of this. ' In connexion with the *Poson* Festival, the Ahimsawardana Society of Wellampitiya has issued 10,000 copies of a pamphlet printed in Sinhalese, asking Buddhists to observe the 14th and 15th instants in a sacred manner, and to abstain from eating flesh and fish on those two days.'[1]

Such appeals as these to Buddhists to abstain from eating flesh on their most sacred days is evidence of the prevalence of flesh-eating amongst them.

The following statement is taken from *The Times of Ceylon*, October 1933 :

' Sir Marcus[2] stated that Mr. Crawford was mistaken when he said that the religious customs of the Buddhists prohibited the eating of beef. There was no such prohibition, and ample proof of this was to be seen in the cases of cattle thefts in the villages where almost invariably the animals were stolen for slaughter. Villagers had a predilection for beef.'

[1] *The Times of Ceylon*, June 14, 1927.
[2] Sir Marcus Fernando, M.D., is an eminent Sinhalese public man.

PART II

VII

BUDDHIST DOCTRINE:

Its Ethics, Psychology and Metaphysics

In the limited space at our disposal we must keep as close to the fundamental principles of Buddhism as possible.

The reader may think that a separate discussion of each of the three subjects given above—Ethics, Psychology, and Metaphysics—would be more helpful than a grouping of them together. But in Buddhism it is impossible to keep them separate one from another, because they overlap at so many points.

The Philosophy of Buddhism is chiefly Psychology, and its Ethics cannot be entirely separated from its Metaphysics. The ultimate purpose of all its philosophy is not intellectual but moral—the attainment of freedom from the pain and unrest of existence, the Buddhist *Summum Bonum*, Nirvana.

We are told in the Pitakas that Gotama Buddha took no interest in purely metaphysical questions; to him they appeared to be questions without profit, and a mere waste of time. Even in his most abstruse teachings his purpose is ethical.

What we are about to attempt is not an exposition of *primitive* Buddhism, but of Buddhist doctrine as it is found in Buddhist books ancient and modern, and as it is accepted and taught by Buddhists today. The materials for writing a satisfactory account of *primitive* Buddhism are not yet available. Even the *Tripitaka*, which undoubtedly contains the oldest traditions which we possess of the Buddha and his teachings, is not entirely reliable, because the most primitive of the books of which it is composed contain the accumulated teachings of generations of Buddhists, and the task of separating the earlier from the later teaching is, at present, an impossible one. (See also p. 19.)

But we are probably justified in thinking that all the great doctrines of Buddhism originated in the teaching of Gotama Buddha, however much they may have been elaborated since his day. We refer to such doctrines as 'The Three Characteristics,' the 'Elements of Being,' 'Karma and Rebirth,' 'Nirvana,' &c.

Buddhists are traditionalists, and seem to have been traditionalists from the very first. They were not likely deliberately to interfere with *the word* of the Buddha. Changes in doctrine probably came imperceptibly. That changes have taken place, no scholar can doubt. For example, no one can accept the elaborate and complicated metaphysical treatises of the Abhidhamma-Pitaka as the original teachings of the Buddha, and the same may be said of much that is found in the Vinaya and Sutta Pitakas, but the roots of all these doctrines probably reach down to the Buddha.

Mrs. C. A. F. Rhys Davids, however, considers (if I understand her aright) that what the world calls Buddhism is an impoverished and devitalized thing, which the Buddha would have repudiated; a product of cloistered monks out of touch with the actual life of men. In a series of books (*Gotama the Man*, *Sakya*, *A Manual of Buddhism*, &c.) she is trying to get behind *the sources* to the *man*, Gotama, and his actual words. I cannot do more here than draw the reader's attention to these books. (See also *The Introduction*, pp. 11–12.)

There is one other point that should be noted here. In reading the Pitakas one is struck with the apparent inconsistencies of the Buddha's teachings. To take one example ;

there is the teaching that what we call *man* is not a living entity or individual, but a *being* made up of the five *Skandhas*, or groups of the ' *constituents of being.*' There is no such thing as a soul, or self, or personality, or individuality in man—no ' Ego ' or *persistent reality* of any kind. This doctrine is graphically, and I think fairly, summarized in the *Visuddhimagga*,[1] Chapter XVI.

> ' Misery only doth exist; none miserable.'
> ' No doer is there; naught but the deed is found.'
> ' Nirvana is, but not the man who seeks it '
> ' The Path exists, but not the traveller on it.'

On the other side, we have the fact that no moral teacher has ever laid greater stress upon the power of an individual to work out his own salvation by his own unaided efforts, than the Buddha. He points to himself as a living example of the truth of his teaching. Millions of years ago he had caught sight of the glorious goal of Nirvana, and he had persistently striven to reach it. Through myriads of lives in various forms of existence, he had pursued his solitary way; through suffering, weariness, and opposition he had pressed on, never wavering, never turning aside, until, at last, under the Bo-tree he had attained his age-long object—Nirvana. And he assured his followers that all who had entered *the path* could reach the goal, as he had reached it. (pp. 53–54.)

The same inconsistency is found in the utterances of modern Buddhist teachers. A learned Buddhist priest, speaking to an audience of Buddhist leaders in Colombo said, amongst other things, the following words :

' Every being is the product of deeds and exists for good and for evil—their legitimate continuation. There is neither a being, nor an individual in reality, but the *Kamma* and consequences, as there is neither doer beyond the deed, nor

[1] Warren, p. 146.

patisanvedanaka : sufferer, beyond consequence; yet for the sake of conventionality we call deed and doer, and consequence and sufferer. Hence the being or doer is delusion; the realities are the deed and the consequence.'

Then the speaker proceeds, toward the close of his address, to give the following practical exhortation :

' The Buddha, our Lord, declares it is *cetana* (will), O Bhikkhus ! I call *Kamma* (deed) because one does every action by thought, word, or body as directed by the will. Now you find the germ of your life either for good or evil depends entirely on your will. When your will is bad and impure all your thoughts, words, and deeds become eventually bad and impure.

' Hence *you must strive hard* to be always pure in your thoughts, words, and deeds, to cultivate in your minds good will not only for your fellow-brethren, but also for all living beings, and to attain Nibbana by following the Noble Eightfold Path.'[1]

I do not wish to comment further on this subject at present, but let the reader bear it in mind, and it will help him to understand much that may appear conflicting, or even contradictory, in the following pages.

The great initial difficulty, for the Western student of Buddhism, is one of mental attitude. He finds it very difficult to approach Buddhism through the eyes and mind of the Buddhist. This is the chief cause of so many misleading books on Buddhism being published in the West. A distinguished scholar has recently reminded us that ' if we are to understand the teaching of Jesus,' we must ' learn to think Semitically.' It is at least equally true that if we are to understand the teaching of Gotama Buddha, we must think ' Buddhistically.'

---

[1] *Sammaditthi,* or ' Right View,' by Suriyagoda Sumangala Thera, B.Lit., Oxon.

We must try to overcome the difficulty of thinking of 'will' without a 'willer'; of 'deed' without a 'doer'; of 'suffering' without a 'sufferer'; in a word, of life being carried on without personal agents. When we have done this, we have taken a big step forward on the path of understanding.

VIII

THE THREE UNIVERSAL TRUTHS

It will help our investigation very materially if, at the very outset, we can grasp for ourselves the fundamental teachings of Buddhism. In the *Anguttara-Nikaya* iii. 134, are set forth what are called 'The Three Characteristics' as follows : ' Whether Buddhas arise, O Priests, or whether Buddhas do not arise, it remains a fact, and the fixed and necessary constitution of *being* that (1) All its constituents are transitory. (2) All its constituents are misery. (3) All its elements are lacking in an Ego. This fact a Buddha discovers and masters, and when he has discovered and mastered it, he announces, teaches, publishes, proclaims, discloses, minutely explains, and makes it clear, that all the constituents of being are transitory, are misery, and are lacking in an Ego.'[1]

Under these three ' characteristics ' or ' universals ' (1) Impermanence (*a-nichcha*) (2) Sorrow or ill (*dukkha*) (3) Absence of an ego, soul, self, individuality, personality, or conscious agent (*anatta*) is included everything that exists whether of matter or mind. Anything outside the three universals is a mere name, like, for example, ' soul ' or ' personality,' which is a convenient designation for the single stream of elements constituting a living being at a given moment of time, though neither the stream itself, nor any single element, nor any combination of elements in the stream is a soul, or contains a soul. Thus the term ' soul ' is but a *name*, and not a *reality*. (For further information see pp. 78–81.)

[1] Warren, p. xiv.

These truths may be regarded as the foundation truths of Buddha's doctrine, and the man who can grasp them is intellectually qualified to become a Buddhist in the stricter sense of the term, and may be expected to master all the doctrines of this profound system sooner or later. He is the 'wise man' of Buddhism in contrast with the generality of men, who, from the Buddhist standpoint, are 'fools.' (See pp. 37–38.)

But all these truths centre round the supreme truth of the universality of suffering. Whilst it is obvious that many of the teachings of the Buddha were the common property of the reflecting religious minds of his day, he made the four sacred truths of suffering peculiarly his own and they became the very kernel and centre of his doctrine.

Though he claims to have acquired great and varied knowledge during his countless rebirths, he was not the Buddha until, under the Bodhi-tree at Uruvela, the four sacred truths dawned upon him, namely that (1) All existence involves suffering; (2) Suffering is caused by desire; especially the desire for continuance of existence; (3) The extinction of desire, therefore, will lead to the extinction of suffering, and (4) The way to this end is the Noble Eightfold Path.

It was the possession of this knowledge which made him the Buddha, the Enlightened One, the Supreme Teacher, and these four truths are the gospel of his newly discovered path of peace. When, after his 'Enlightenment,' he went to the Deer Park at Benares, and preached his doctrine to the five ascetics, with whom he had once lived and practised austerities, this was the substance of his preaching; indeed these four truths were the centre and heart of all his preaching to the end of his life. (See p. 51.) Gotama makes it clear that, but for the fact of sorrow in the universe, there would have been no need for the Supreme Buddha to have appeared in the world at all.

For example, he says, 'If these three things were not in the world, my disciples, the Perfect One, the holy supreme Buddha would not appear in the world; What three things are they? Birth and old age and death.'[1] He goes on to say that no Samana, nor any Brahman, or any god, neither Mara, nor Brahma, nor any being in the universe, can save any living creature from these dreaded experiences. Hence the need for the Buddha to show the way of deliverance.

Other Indian teachers of Buddha's day held this conception of life as sorrow. One writer has said 'What the Indian fears is not death—kindly beneficent death—but life, life, which keeps on endlessly renewing itself through ceaseless rebirths—that is the one spectre of horror that haunts the Indian mind.' Pessimism was widespread, and the people, especially the rich and great, were weary of life, and had no hope either in this world or in any other. But with other teachers this doctrine of suffering was not supreme; they were also deeply interested in the individual soul, and the great All-Soul. They speculated about the gods and had many intellectual interests.

With Gotama Buddha it was not so. God and the universe interested him not at all; he believed neither in the individual soul, nor in the Universal Soul.[2] Speculations about the unknown seemed to him a waste of time and energy—things without profit. He knew only one question, 'How shall I, in this world of suffering, be delivered from suffering?' The one thing that he

---

[1] *Anguttara-Nikaya*, Vol. III, quoted in Oldenberg's *Buddha*, p. 217.

[2] It has been suggested, ' on *a priori* grounds, that Gotama was unlikely to have broken so radically from all Indian tradition as to preach atheism, and soullessness in the way attributed to him.' That may be so. But, so far as I am aware, the Buddha is nowhere represented in the Pitakas as referring to God (*Brahman-Atman*). Though he must have been well acquainted with this Hindu belief, he quietly ignored it. He believed in the Hindu *gods*, as all his contemporaries did, but those gods were phenomenal beings, and, like men, subject to death and rebirth.

regarded as certain and indisputable was the fact of Universal Sorrow.

He calmly surveyed the world of men and saw only sorrow. Then he turned his attention to the heavens of the gods and to the realms where dwelt all other living beings : but he perceived everywhere sorrow and pain from which there was no escape—not even in the heaven of the highest gods. To him there appeared to be only one thing worth striving for—freedom from sorrow; that was his sacred goal.

Let no one suppose that Gotama Buddha's conception of sorrow was merely intellectual and visionary. (Just vague *world-sorrow*.) Few have realized sorrow in so human a way as a thing of pain and dread which expresses itself in tears and agony.

In the *Samyutta-Nikaya*, Text ii. 180,[1] the Buddha is represented as saying :

' Pilgrimage (*Samsara*) of beings, my disciples, has its beginning in eternity. No opening can be discovered from which proceeding creatures, mazed in ignorance, fettered by a thirst for being, stray and wander. What think ye, disciples, whether is more, the water which is in the four great oceans, or the tears which have flowed from you and have been shed by you, while ye strayed and wandered in this long pilgrimage ? '

Then he goes on to speak of disappointments and losses in life after life, of bereavements—the deaths of father, mother, brothers and sisters, sons, daughters. ' All this have ye experienced through long ages.'

The Buddha, then, begins with the great fact of Universal Sorrow, in which all living beings are involved, whether men, brutes, demons, or gods. As outward and visible manifestations of this sorrow, the Buddha sees Birth, Disease, Old Age, Death, Rebirth—these are the terrible powers of destruction which hover over life. But why should sorrow, pain, misery reign supreme in the universe ?

[1] See *Kindred Sayings*, Vol. II, pp. 118-25.

The Buddha replies : Because there is no permanence, everything is transitory ; there is no ' being,' only ' becoming.' In living beings, and in inanimate things, there is nothing that abides—all are perishable, everything is changing, there is no rest, no peace, no satisfaction in aught that is, or can be thought to be ; and only where there is no change can there be no sorrow—change and sorrow are mere cause and effect. ' Behind every blossoming forth there is a fading, behind every attainment a loss, behind every life, death.'

Stcherbatsky, speaking of *dukkha*, says ; ' The idea underlying it is that the elements described above are perpetually in a state of commotion, and the ultimate goal of the world process consists in their gradual appeasement and final extinction. The old Buddhist credo (*ye dharmā hetu-prabhavāḥ*) already expresses the idea very sharply : " the Great Recluse has indicated the (separate) elements, their inter-connexion as causes and effects, and their final suppression." '[1]

We see how, in the Buddha's thought, transitoriness and misery, impermanence and sorrow, were inevitably bound together. Buddha not only taught that there is misery in the world—that this or that thing is evil ; but that, in the very nature and constitution of things no good is anywhere possible, inasmuch as the ' three characteristics (1. transitoriness, 2. misery, 3. the lack of an ego) inhere in all things.' In the next chapter we shall examine the Buddha's Doctrine of Man.

[1] *The Central Conception of Buddhism*, p. 48. See also *Sariputta's Teaching*, p. 97.

IX

THE BUDDHIST DOCTRINE OF MAN

WE HAVE shown in the last chapter that Gotama Buddha built up his Philosophy on the foundation truth of the Universality of Suffering. It is necessary, however, continually to bear in mind that the Doctrine of suffering and misery arises out of the teacher's belief that all things in this world, and in every known and conceivable world, are transitory and impermanent. This doctrine applies equally to living beings, and to inanimate things. There is nothing that corresponds to our idea of ' substance ' (' no underlying persistent reality,' as Warren phrases it) in material things. And in living beings, including man, there is no permanent element, physical or spiritual, that will survive the death of the body.

This belief and teaching was not peculiar to Gotama Buddha, but, according to Buddhist tradition, it was the common belief of all former Buddhas, and would be believed and taught by all the Buddhas who might appear in the world in future ages. In the introduction of the Jataka we read observations upon the right times, and the times which are not right, for a Buddha to appear in the world. ' Now it is not the right time when the length of men's lives is more than a hundred thousand years. And why is it not the right time ? Because mortals then forget about birth, old age, and death. And if the Buddhas, who always include in their teaching the Three Characteristics, were to attempt, at such a time, to discourse concerning *transitoriness*, *misery*, and *the lack of a substantive reality*, men

would not think it worth while listening to them, nor would
they give them credence.'[1]

Such conversations as the following meet us again and
again in early Buddhist writings :

' What think you, brother Yamaka ? Is form permanent
or transitory ? '

' It is transitory, brother.'

' And that which is transitory, is it evil, or is it good ? '

' It is evil, brother.'

' And that which is transitory, evil, and liable to change,
is it possible to say of it : " This is mine ; this am I ; this
is my Ego " ? '

' Nay, verily, brother.'[2]

Seeing that this doctrine of ' Transitoriness ' forms the
back-ground of all Buddha's teaching and colours all his
thought, there is great need to keep it in mind—especially
in our present examination of the Buddha's doctrine of man.

According to Buddhism, every sentient thing, including
man, is made up of five groups of elements called *Skandhas*.
These five groups are briefly described as *Nama-rupa*, that
is, ' name and form,' or ' mind and matter.' This is an old
Hindu, pre-Buddhistic, term which was taken over by
Gotama Buddha.

The idea of *matter* (*rupa*) in Buddhism is very hard to
grasp. It is divided into two categories : (1) objective
sense-data, constituting external objects and (2) sense organs
conceived of as a kind of translucent subtle *matter* which
covers the body when it is living. Briefly, matter is mere
sense-data without any substance. External matter is
' manifested by the facts of hardness or repulsion, cohesion
or attraction, heat and motion. Conventionally these four
elements are called earth, water, fire and air. They appear
always together, always in equal proportion. There is as

[1] Warren, pp. 38–40.
[2] *Samyutta-Nikaya*, XXII, 85[1], Warren, p. 140.

much element of heat in a blazing flame as there is in wood or water, and vice versa, the difference is only in their intensity.'[1]

The term ' *nama* ' covers the other four groups of elements ; (2) feelings ; (3) ideas ; (4) volitions and other faculties, and (5) pure sensation or general Consciousness.[2]

There is a second more detailed classification of the elements called *Ayatanas*. (' The word, *Ayatana*, means simply place or sphere for meeting or of origin, or ground of happening, it is used to cover *both* organ of sense and sense-object. The meeting is that effected between organ of sense and sense-object.')[3] The *Ayatanas* are made up of the five physical senses and consciousness, and of the five objects of sense, together with non-sensuous objects which can be perceived only by intellect or consciousness.

The twelve *Ayatanas*, or bases of cognition, may be tabulated in two groups of six :

1. *The six receptive faculties.*

1. Sense of vision.   4. Sense of taste.
2. Sense of hearing.   5. Sense of touch.
3. Sense of smelling.   6. Faculty of intellect or consciousness.

2. *The six objects of the senses and consciousness.*

7. Colour and Shape.   10. Taste.
8. Sound.   11. Touchable things.
9. Odour.   12. Non-sensuous objects.

' In this classification (*Ayatanas*) the eleven first items correspond to eleven elements (*dharma*) each including one. The twelfth item contains all the remaining sixty-four

---

[1] *The Central Conception of Buddhism*, p. 13.

[2] The Pali terms for these five groups are: *rupa, vedana, sanna, sankhara,* and *vinnana*.

[3] Mrs. Rhys Davids, *Buddhist Psychology*, p. 57.

elements, and it is therefore called *dharma-ayatana* or simply *dharmah*, i.e. the remaining elements.'[1]

The ordinary man is made up of 72 elements. The remaining three belong to the perfect saint alone.[2]

Consciousness is said to be pure sensation, without any content. It must not be confused with what western thinkers call *mind*, which is active. Therefore consciousness never arises alone, but must always be supported by two elements : one of the senses and an object of sense. Thus visual consciousness is made up of pure consciousness, together with the sense of vision, and an object of vision, some colour or shape. ' Consciousness is further defined as " awareness," in every single case (of what is now present to the senses, or to the mind directly).'[3]

Consciousness appears to be like a mirror which simply reflects whatever is brought in front of it.

There is a third division of the elements of existence into eighteen *dhatus*, made up of the twelve *ayatanas*, together with the six kinds of consciousness, as follows :

13. Consciousness of sight.
14. Consciousness of hearing.
15. Consciousness of smelling.
16. Consciousness of taste.
17. Consciousness of touch.
18. Consciousness of non-sensuous objects.

We cannot pursue this subject into greater detail here, but the following books are specially commended :

(1) *The Central Conception of Buddhism*, by Th. Stcherbatsky, Ph.D., published by The Royal Asiatic Society.

---

[1] *The Central Conception of Buddhism*, pp. 7, 8.
[2] ibid., pp. 71-72. These are space and two *nirodhas* or cessations : 1, cessation by comprehension of the truths ; 2, cessation, not through knowledge, but by extinction of the cause, as when fire goes out.
[3] Mrs. Rhys Davids, *Buddhist Psychology*, p. 70.

(2) *Buddhist Psychology*, by Mrs. C. A. F. Rhys Davids.

I am mainly indebted to these two writers for the notes given above.

The point to be especially noted here is that the Buddha emphatically and absolutely denied the presence of a ' Soul,' or ' Self,' or ' Ego ' in man. Gotama Buddha regarded the belief in an ' Ego,' a ' Self,' an ' Individuality ' which differentiates one from others and from the universe at large, as the most persistent delusion of gods and men. As we read in the *Samyutta-Nikaya*, xii. 62 :

' And the blessed One spoke as follows : " Even the ignorant unconverted man, O priests, may conceive an aversion for this body, which is composed of the four elements, may divest himself of passion for it, and attain to freedom from it. And why do I say so ? Because, O priests, the increase and wasting away of this body, which is composed of the four elements, are evident, and the way in which it is obtained and afterwards laid away again. But that, O priests, which is called ' mind, intellect, conscious-ness '—here the ignorant, unconverted man is not equal to conceiving aversion, to divesting himself of passion, to attaining freedom. And why do I say so ? Because, O priests, from time immemorial the ignorant, unconverted man has held, cherished, and affected the notion ' This is mine ; this am I ; this is my Ego.' But it were better, O priests, if the ignorant unconverted man regarded the body, which is composed of the four elements, as an ' Ego ' rather than the mind. And why do I say so ? Because it is evident, O priests, that the body lasts one year, three years, twenty years, fifty years, a hundred years, and even more. But that, O priests, which is called mind, intellect, con-sciousness, keeps up an incessant round by day and by night of perishing as one thing, and springing up as another." '[1]

[1] Warren, pp. 150-51.

The meaning of the above quotation is clear, and needs little comment. If a man could only believe that the body is the ' Ego,' the ' Self,' it would be easy to persuade him that such a body is unworthy of his loving regard, and he, being willing to give it up, would cease to cling to existence. But when a man conceives the ' Ego ' to be the dwelling place of the mind, the affections, the will, and all the intellectual and spiritual powers, he regards it as something very precious. He says ' this is I, this is mine, my very self,' and he cleaves to it and is very loath to let it go. This attachment to the ' Ego,' to the individuality, is the greatest hindrance to the Buddhist's religious progress—it is the strong chain which binds him to existence, and, until this chain is snapped, there is no hope of final deliverance.

Therefore, the Buddha strove unceasingly to persuade his followers that, whilst the body is but temporary and will pass away, the mind is even more impermanent and evanescent, for the body indeed changes comparatively slowly, but the mind is never the same for two consecutive moments—it is ever in a state of flux, having no underlying reality at all. Like that optical toy, the kaleidoscope, in which, as we shake it, we see an endless variety of beautiful colours and forms, but never the same combination twice, however long we shake it, so the mind of the present or future is never identical with the mind of any moment in past time.

The Pitakas represent Gotama Buddha as holding firmly to the belief that there is no continuous personal identity. Many passages from the early books might be quoted to show that his followers have shared this belief with him ; but the following short extract from the writings of the learned Buddhaghosa will meet the case. ' Strictly speaking, the duration of the life of a living being is exceedingly brief, lasting only while a thought lasts. Just as a chariot wheel in rolling rolls only at one point of the tyre, and in resting rests only at one point; in exactly the same way, the life of a living being lasts only for the period of one thought. As soon as that thought has ceased the being is said to have ceased. As it has been said :

" The being of the past moment of thought has lived, but does not live, nor will it live."

" The being of a future moment of thought will live, but has not lived, nor does it live."

" The being of the present moment of thought does live, but has not lived, nor will it live." [1]

Perhaps the clearest statements, in ancient Buddhist writings, of the doctrine that there is in man no ' Soul ' or ' Ego ' are to be found in *The Questions of King Milinda*. This book records (supposed) discussions on profound religious subjects between the great Buddhist saint and teacher Nagasena, and the Greek King Menander, or Milinda (about 100 B.C.). The following is a very condensed account of the discussion on the soul, from T. W. Rhys Davids' Translation, pp. 40–45. [2] No summary, however, can give such a strong impression of Nagasena's belief in the absolute negation of a soul in man, as one receives from reading the whole discussion.

And Milinda began by asking ' What Sir, is your name ? ' ' I am known as Nagasena, O King. But although parents gave such a name as Nagasena, it is only a generally understood term, a designation in common use. For there is no permanent individuality (no soul) involved in the matter.'

Then Milinda said to those present, ' This Nagasena says there is no permanent individuality (no soul) implied in his name. Is it now even possible to approve him in that?' And turning to Nagasena, he said, ' If, most reverend Nagasena, there be no permanent individuality (no soul) in the matter, who is it who lives a life of righteousness ?

[1] Warren, *Visuddhimagga*, Chap. VIII, p. 150.
[2] *Sacred Books of the East*, Vol. XXXV.

Who is it who devotes himself to meditations ? Who attains to the Nirvana of Arahantship ? If that be so, there is neither merit nor demerit : there is neither doer nor causer of good or evil deeds ; there is neither fruit nor result of good or evil Karma. If, most reverend Nagasena, we are to think that were a man to kill you there would be no murder, then it follows, that there are no real masters or teachers of your Order, and that your ordinations are void.' Then follows the well-known comparison between Naga-sena and the Chariot.

Again we quote from the same book pp. 132–33. ' The King said : " These three, Nagasena—perception, and reason, and the soul in a being—are they all different both in letter and in essence, or the same in essence differing only in letter ? "

' " Recognition, O King, is the mark of perception, and discrimination of reason, and there is no such thing as a soul in beings." '

' But if there be no such thing as a soul, what is it then which sees forms with the eye, and hears sounds with the ear, and smells odours with the nose, and tastes tastes with the tongue, and feels touch with the body or perceives qualities with the mind ?

' The elder replied : " If there be a soul (distinct from the body) which does all this, then if the eye were plucked out could it stretch out its head, as it were, through the larger aperture and see forms much more clearly than before ? Could one hear sounds better if the ears were torn away, or smell better if the nose were cut off, or taste better if the tongue were pulled out, or feel better if the body were destroyed ? "

' " Certainly not, sir."

' " Then there can be no soul inside the body."

' " Very good, Nagasena ! " '

Clearer evidence than the above quotations that Gotama

Buddha and his early disciples denied the existence of a soul in man, cannot be desired. The suggestion that Gotama did not use the word 'Soul' and 'Ego' in the modern sense will not bear examination. He understood perfectly well what rival teachers meant by the transmigration of the soul. We will therefore add only one short selection from the *Visuddhimagga* Chapter XVIII.[1] and another from a modern Buddhist writer and then bring this investigation to an end.

'The words "living entity" or "Ego" are but a mode of expression for the presence of the five attachment groups, but when we come to examine the elements one by one we discover that, in the absolute sense, there is no "living entity" there to form a basis for such figments as "I am" or "I"; in other words, that in the absolute sense, there is only "Name" and "Form." The insight of him who perceives this is called "knowledge of the truth."'

Perhaps someone will say. 'But, after all, what is the use of discussing this ancient Buddhist teaching about man? Nobody holds these views today.' On the contrary, these are the views held by learned Buddhist priests, and intelligent Buddhist laymen at the present time. The following extract from an article on 'Buddhism in the West' by J. E. Ellam[2] published in *The Buddhist Annual of Ceylon*, 1921, must suffice, though quotations from modern Buddhist writers could be multiplied if space permitted.

'The Buddhist analysis of man's being into the five *khandhas* (*skandhas*) is exactly in accordance with scientific monism. The body (*rupa*, the vehicle) we know to be made up of elements which are in a constant process of flux. . . . It is the same with the rapid changes of sensation, perception, consciousness, and the mental properties (*sankhara*); which last, if anything, might be called the "soul," since

[1] Warren, pp. 133-34.
[2] Associate Editor, *Buddhist Review*, London.

it is here that the illusion of the self-separate " Ego " arises. This has been aptly likened to a flame, a shifting iridescence. . . . Never for one fraction of a second is it still, or at rest. This is the " I," the " self," what men call the " soul." Immortal ? It is so mortal that one moment's time can hardly span its life. The body (*rupa*) is less mortal than the " soul." '

Although Buddhists deny the existence of a *person*, or an *individual*, as an ultimate reality, they acknowledge that there are *individual streams* of existence which are distinct from all other such *streams*. The individual stream is made up of all the mental and physical elements of the individual mind and body, together with such external objects as enter into the consciousness at any given moment. But this *stream* is never the same for two consecutive moments ; it is like the kaleidoscope, to which reference has already been made. (See pp. 76–77.)

This stream is held together, kept in its course as one might say, by a special force, called *prapti*. Moreover, it has flowed out unbrokenly from past existences, and it will flow on beyond this life into future existences. It is often compared to a river of which an ignorant man might say ; ' This river has been here for hundreds of years,' but the intelligent man knows that not one drop of water which he now sees ever passed this way before, or will ever pass again—the stream is ever coming and passing away.

So it is with the individual stream of life. It is often compared to the flame of a lamp which is in a state of continual unrest and change. But perhaps the most perfect illustration is that of the cinema picture. To the onlooker it appears to be continuous, but it is, in fact, made up of a great number of pictures following one another on the screen with such rapidity that the eye is deceived.

But even the ordinary cinema picture is not a perfect illustration of the *stream of existence*, because the picture represents continuous action on the part of the actors. For we are told that one moment of existence in the *stream* does not arise out of the preceding moment of existence as an effect from a cause. ' A cause for the Buddhists is not a real cause, but a preceding moment, which likewise arose out of nothing in order to disappear into nothing. Consequently the elements do not change but disappear. Disappearance is of the very essence of existence ; for what does not disappear does not exist.'[1]

Thus the Buddhist theory of *becoming* and *passing away* is not really a theory of cause and effect. The elements of being are all independent entities, existing of and by themselves and not in dependence, one upon another. ' The elements of existence are momentary appearances, momentary flashings into the phenomenal world out of an unknown source. They are not connected one with another. They disappear as soon as they appear, in order to be followed the next moment by another momentary existence. Thus a moment becomes a synonym of an element (*dharma*), two moments are two different elements. An element becomes something like a point in time-space.'[2]

Thus the most perfect illustration of the *stream of existence* is a cinema picture,[3] which is made up of thousands of individual drawings, each separate and distinct, but following one another on the screen with such quickness that the illusion of continuity is produced. Thus every flashing moment in the life stream, which is all that Buddhists recognize as *personality* or *individuality*, is distinct from and independent of every preceding and every following moment. This is evidently a later scholastic development and elaboration of the Buddha's primitive doctrine of ' becoming and passing away,' but it seems to be a legitimate development.

[1] *The C.C. of Buddhism*, p. 38.
[2] ibid., p. 37.
[3] Such as ' Mickey Mouse.'

D

It follows that the Buddha, denying the existence of the soul, has no doctrine of the transmigration of the soul, such as that which is universally held by Hindus. To Indian thought ' One existence follows another in an unbroken chain and the " soul " is the thread that binds them together.' Buddhism, however, substitutes for transmigration, the doctrine of ' a round of rebirths.' But how is rebirth possible if no soul, or other permanent element, remains over at death to furnish a link between one existence and the next ? An attempt will be made to answer this question in the next chapter.

X

KARMA AND REBIRTH

Or the Buddha's Teaching about the Future Life

THE BUDDHA taught clearly and persistently that, though there is no living entity in man, which will survive the death of the body, Karma (the good and evil fruits of his actions) survives. We may say therefore that in the Buddha's thought Karma took the place of the soul in man and made Rebirth possible. It is evident that the doctrine of Karma is vital to the Buddha's system of philosophy, and demands our closest attention.

This doctrine is not peculiar to Buddhism. Gotama brought it over with him from Hinduism, where it is always associated with Transmigration. A brief inquiry into the origin and development of the doctrine of transmigration will clear difficulties and misunderstandings out of the way, and make it easier to comprehend the Buddha's more intricate and involved theory of ' Rebirth without Transmigration.'

Belief in the Transmigration of the Soul can be traced back to the childhood of our race. Moreover, it appears to have arisen independently in many different ages and lands. This doctrine is found in its simplest form amongst certain savage tribes, who believe that the soul at death has to find a new dwelling-place, and, though it generally takes possession of the body of an infant, may be driven to find refuge in an animal.

Among some African tribes there is a belief that usually the soul of an ancestor reanimates the body of an infant

amongst his descendants. 'The Yoruba negroes greet a
new-born child with the words " Thou art come," and then
decide which ancestral soul has returned.'

Similar beliefs are held by Red Indians in America, and
by the 'Blacks' of Australia. The latter regarded white
men as reincarnations of their (the 'Blacks') ancestors—
a sort of ghosts.[1]

A more clearly defined and elaborated theory of transmigration was found amongst certain highly civilized and
cultured peoples. For instance it is probable that the
ancient Egyptians believed in the transmigration of souls,
and this doctrine was clearly taught by Pythagoras and Plato
amongst the Greeks. But this theory was merely a philosophical speculation, which was never generally adopted
by the Greeks.

Though the theory of transmigration is so widespread, it
does not appear to have been held by the early Aryans.
There is no trace of it in the *Vedas*, which is fairly sound
evidence that the Aryans did not bring it to India with
them. We find it first in the *Upanishads*, and we may assume
with some confidence that the invading Aryans adopted
this theory from the aboriginal peoples of North India.

At that time, in all probability, the moral element—the
idea of retribution—would be either absent or only very
feebly developed in the theory. There was a conviction
common to the early Aryans, however, that the world is a
moral world, and that justice is at the foundation of all
things.

Yet life, as they knew it, appeared to be unjust—the
inequalities were too apparent, and there seemed to be a great
deal of unmerited suffering in the world. It was not only
that evil men suffered, but the virtuous were grievously
afflicted, and often the victims of great calamities.

[1] For a wealth of information on this subject see articles under *Metem-
psychosis, Reincarnation, Transmigration,* in *E.R.E. Indexes*, p. 378.

It was suggested that the answer to these painful and pressing questions must be sought, not in the present life, but in a previous existence. If it were possible to believe that men were now receiving the rewards and punishments due to their deeds in former lives, then abstract justice would be satisfied—for this theory would explain the actual disproportion of suffering to relative merit amongst men. In some such way, in all probability, the doctrine of Karma arose. The doctrine of transmigration alone would have failed to satisfy the mind and heart of a moral people, such as the early Aryans were, but when it was strengthened by the belief in Karma, the combined doctrine gripped both the imagination of men and their moral consciousness.

The doctrine of Karma, therefore, is probably not the product of the abstract reasonings of philosophers, but arose amongst ordinary intelligent people out of the problem of suffering. This theory, indeed, can be made to explain anything. Is a man born blind, or deaf, or in abject poverty ? It is the result of his Karma. Is a woman ugly, ill-natured, and despised ? It is the result of her Karma. (See p. 89.) There is no problem in life that this theory will not solve, and, by its very nature, it is itself incapable of experimental proof or disproof. We need not wonder, therefore, that this theory of life is so attractive to many practical men, who do not care to search far below the surface of things.

But note carefully that, according to the Hindu theory, the soul—the real man—passed from existence to existence, bearing always with him his Karma—the good and evil consequences of his deeds in former lives. According to Hindu thought the body is of little account, but the soul is of supreme importance. It is the soul that sins and suffers endlessly, unless, indeed, through retributive suffering, meritorious deeds and, above all, through knowledge it attains unto absorption into the *Brahman-Atman*. This theory is not difficult to understand, and it appeals, perhaps, more to the practical man, living the common life of man, face to face with its perplexities and tragedies, than to the philosopher in his isolated thought-world.

But when we come to the consideration of Gotama Buddha's doctrine of Karma and Rebirth, we find ourselves in the presence of a theory of life much more difficult to understand and to explain, for here there is no living soul to connect each life with the next, or to act as the dwelling place and agent of Karma. The Buddha teaches that, just as during life the only persistent reality in man is his Karma, so at death, when the elements of being are dissolved, nothing remains over but Karma—i.e. the abstract consequences of action—and this is the only connecting link between the individuals of a series of existences which extends backward through millions of years, and will continue for millions more in the future, i.e. an Infinite and Eternal Series. (See pp. 91–93.)

There was always, amongst Buddhists, a strong temptation to believe that ' Consciousness ' (*vinnana*) passes from the dying man to the newly conceived *embryo* in which his *Karma* must work itself out, and there appears to be some support for the theory in the Pitakas. For example, we find in the *Digha-N.* ii. 63 the following passage (where the Buddha is represented as questioning Ananda):

' Were *vinnana* (consciousness) Ananda, not to descend into the mother's womb, would body and mind become constituted therein ? ' The answer is, ' No, they would not.'[1]

Mrs. Rhys Davids suggests that a folklore speech has here got into the *Suttanta* teaching, because, ' For Buddhists the dissolution of the factors of a living individual at death was complete,' and this is the almost unanimous teaching of the Buddhist *Canon*, as well as of later books.[2]

---

[1] Quoted by Mrs. Rhys Davids in *Buddhist Psychology*, p. 22.
[2] But see also *Samyutta-N*, II. 13, 91, 101.

Mrs. Rhys Davids quotes another passage from the sayings of the Buddha, which, while throwing light on the prevalence of the theory that 'Consciousness is reincarnated in the new *embryo*,' would seem finally to dispose of the theory.

A bhikkhu, Sāti Fisher-son, gives out as the Buddha's own teaching that 'It is mind (*vinnana*) which persists and is reborn after death unchanged.' He is summoned to repeat this before the Master. 'Is it true, Sati, that you said this?' 'Yea, lord, so do I understand you to teach.' 'What, Sati, is this mind?' 'That speaker, that feeler, lord, who experiences the results of good and evil deeds done here or there.'

'Now then, foolish man, whence got you such a doctrine as being teaching of mine? Have I not taught you by many methods that mind arises from a cause; and except from a cause, mind cannot come to be?'

The bhikkhus bear him out in this.[1]

The reader must carefully avoid the common mistake of regarding Transmigration and Rebirth as practically identical. The two theories are essentially different. Buddhism teaches Rebirth without Transmigration, as the following extract from 'The Questions of King Milinda' will show:[2]

The king said: 'Where there is no transmigration, Nagasena, can there be rebirth?'

'Yes, there can.'

'But how can that be? Give me an illustration.'

'Suppose a man, O king, were to light a lamp from another lamp, can it be said that one transmigrates from, or to, the other?'

'Certainly not.'

---

[1] *Majjhima-N.* i, 256 ff, *Buddhist Psychology*, p. 15, and *S.B.B.*, Vol. V, pp. 183-85. For a careful discussion of 'consciousness' in relation to *Rebirth*, see Oldenberg's *Buddha*, pp. 227-31.

[2] T. W. Rhys Davids, *S.B.E.*, Vol. XXXV, pp. 111-12.

' Just so, great king, is rebirth without transmigration.'

The king said : ' Is there any being, Nagasena, who transmigrates from this body to another ? '

' No, there is not.'

' But if so, would it not get free from its evil deeds ? '

' Yes, if it were not reborn, but if it were, no. This name-and-form commits deeds, either pure or impure, and by that Karma another name-and-form is reborn, and therefore it is not set free from its evil deeds.'

The teaching in the above quotation is so clear that it does not call for further elucidation ; but the doctrine itself is very difficult to grasp. The reader may well ask, ' Why is all life subject to the dread control of Karma ? Who has ordained that Karma shall bring into existence new beings to suffer the penal consequences of previously existing creatures' lives ? By whose will has the universe been so constituted ? ' The Buddhist reply is that there is no ' Supreme Will ' in the universe—no Creator or personal First Cause, but things happen according to the law of cause and effect, or, more correctly, by the law of ' Dependent Origination.' As a writer in *The Buddhist Annual of Ceylon*, 1921, says :

' There is no room here for childish " Creation " stories, for, as the Buddha knew, there was no creation. Hence the doctrine of Dependent Origination (*Paticca-Sammuppada*) so much misunderstood by Western students of Buddhism. The doctrine of " Dependent Origination " does away with the theory of a necessary First Cause. As there is infinity in time and space, so there is infinity in sequence of cause and effect. Each cycle is but the successor of that which went before, and this cycle will be followed by others. They are simply the cycles of the *Samsara* (the sequence of the arising, transition, decay, passing away, and re-arising of beings), eternal except for one possibility,' i.e. the attainment of Nirvana. We cannot here attempt a detailed explanation of the Buddhist doctrine of Dependent Origination.[1]

It is enough for our present purpose to know that Karma lies at the very heart of the doctrine, i.e. the world undergoes periodic dissolution and re-formation in order that Karma may have a field in which to work itself out.

We will now define, a little more in detail, what Gotama Buddha meant by Karma. His idea of Karma is that life in quality as well as in quantity is strictly determined by the deeds of a previous existence.

The following points must be especially noted:

1. He regarded retribution as personal.[2] A man reaps exactly what he has sown, even though it takes an eternity of lives in which to reap the harvest. No God, or man, or any other power in the universe, can mitigate the suffering, or save a man from the full consequences of his deeds in pain or pleasure.

2. A man is not merely punished to the full for his evil deeds, but the punishment is also made to fit the crime—it is always appropriate in quality and quantity. This is shown very clearly in the Birth Stories. For example, in the story of Queen Mallika, the Queen inquired from Gotama why she was ugly, of a bad figure, and horrible to look at, and yet wealthy and high in the social scale.

The Buddha replied, ' When a woman has been irascible and violent, and at every little thing said against her has felt spiteful, enraged, and sulky, and manifested hatred and heart-burning, but has given alms to monks and Brahmans, and has not been of an envious disposition, then whenever she leaves that existence and comes to this one, wherever she may be born, she is ugly, of a bad figure, and horrible to look at, and rich, affluent, and high in the social scale.'[3]

[1] But see Mrs. Rhys Davids, *Buddhism*, pp. 90-91.
[2] In Buddhism this is regarded as true, notwithstanding all that has been said about ' non-existence of personality ' in man. See pp. 63, 64, 65, 93-94.
[3] *Anguttara-N.*, IV, 197[1], condensed from ' Warren ', pp. 228-31.

3. A being cannot expiate its demerits by deeds of merit. It is a mistake to suppose that 'Evil' Karma can be balanced by 'Good,' that at the end of life a balance sheet is drawn up, in which the final balance may be one of merit or demerit. Merit and demerit are always separate and distinct. They work themselves out to their final consequences quite independently.

This is illustrated in the story quoted above and much more clearly in 'The Death of Moggallana.' Though Moggallana had fulfilled the seven perfections, and had become one of the greatest disciples of the Buddha, and had attained to *enlightenment*, so that after this life he would no more be reborn, but would pass into Nirvana, yet, because in a former life, hundreds of thousands of years before, he had committed a particularly diabolical and atrocious crime (the crime of cruelly deceiving his blind and helpless parents, and beating them to death, all the time pretending that they were being beaten by robbers), he himself was beaten to death by robbers, and all his bones were broken to the size of rice grains.

When the news reached the Buddha's other disciples they said, ' Moggallana the Great met with a death unworthy of him.' The Buddha replied, ' Priests, the death of Moggallana the Great was unsuited to his present existence, but suited to his Karma of a previous existence.' And he told them the story given above.[1]

4. Good Karma, just as much as Evil Karma, must work itself out. Therefore to escape rebirth one must cease from good as well as evil deeds. We will consider this more at length when we are dealing with the doctrine of Nirvana.

Though the Buddha taught the fact of Rebirth clearly and emphatically, he does not appear ever to have attempted to explain the doctrine to his followers. They were origin-

---

[1] *Dhammapada*, pp. 298-301, ' Warren,' pp. 221-26.

ally believers in the existence of a soul which transmigrates from body to body. This new teaching that no soul exists, and that Rebirth takes place without transmigration, was as puzzling to them as it is to us. They frequently questioned the Buddha on this subject : they wanted a rational explanation of how Rebirth took place without a soul.

The question arose in their minds, ' If nothing in body or mind has, or is, soul (self, *atta*), what soul is there to be affected by deeds which no soul has done ? ' This very reasonable question is characterized by the Buddha as the idea of ' a futile person ' of one who ' still is ignorant, under the influence of craving, straying from the Teacher's doctrine.'[1]

Instead of attempting to give an answer to this question, ' If there be no soul how can there be consequences of deeds, and who will suffer those consequences ? ' he attempts to divert the questioner's attention to something else, namely, the impossibility of an impermanent body or mind being a soul. This is the Buddha's usual method of evading this question. (See pp. 71–72.)

If we may judge from the *Tripitaka*, he never met this question fairly, or attempted to answer it. The result is that all generations of Buddhists, down to our own days, have been bewildered by this doctrine. Many attempts have been made to explain it in a rational way, but with little, if any, success. To his personal disciples the doctrine of Karma and Rebirth was a mysterious dogma of the Buddha which had to be accepted by a supreme act of unquestioning faith. Present-day Buddhists regard it as a mystery which ordinary mortals cannot be expected to understand.

The great Buddhist Commentator, Buddhaghosa, in the *Visuddhimagga*, attempts to explain *Rebirth* in the following terms :

[1] *Majjhima-N*, III, 19ff. *S.B.B.*, Vol. VI, pp. 166-67.

'He who has no clear idea of death, or of rebirth, and does not master the fact that death is the dissolution of the five factors (mind and body), and that rebirth is the appearance of the five factors, he concludes that "a living entity deceases and transmigrates into another body" or "a living entity is reborn and has got a new body" . . . no elements of being transmigrate from the last existence into the present, nor do they appear in the present existence without causes in the past existence.

'For at the hour of death the last conscious act is as a man who, to cross a ditch, swings himself over by a rope hung up on a tree above him. Yet he does not really alight, for while the last conscious act dies away (and this is called "passing away") another conscious act arises in a new life, and this is called "rebirth" or conception. *But it is to be understood that the latter conscious act did not come into the present life from the previous life*. We must also understand that it is only to causes contained in the old existence that its present appearance is due.'[1]

The Buddhist doctrine of rebirth is stated very clearly in the above extract. There is the emphatic denial that 'a living entity deceases and transmigrates into another body' or that 'a living entity is reborn and has got a new body,' whilst the new 'becoming' is represented as due to the last act of consciousness of the dying predecessor, even consciousness does not pass over, 'does not alight'— nothing passes over except 'Karma.'

Mrs. Rhys Davids commenting on this passage says, 'The last mental or conscious act, just when the body is ceasing to act as a living nucleus *pro tem.*, is an act of transitive causation, like its predecessors. And it transmits its *pachchaya-satti*, or causal energy so runs the hypothesis—to some newly conceived embryonic germ, human or non-human. To answer the question: "In *which* new embryo

[1] Mrs. Rhys Davids, *Buddhism*, p. 144.

does any given final flicker of mental *kamma* produce its effect ? " no materials containing any Buddhist theories on the subject are yet available, either medieval or modern.'[1]

Buddhist writers of the present day are deeply concerned about this mystery. They claim that Buddhism is, above all else, a *rational* system, and it is very irksome not to be able to give a rational explanation of the central Buddhist Doctrine of Karma and Rebirth. Perhaps the best modern attempt at an explanation is that made by the learned Buddhist Monk, Silacara Bhikkhu. I will quote his own words :

' In the self-same way, the now-being, which is the present manifestation of the stream of Kamma-energy, *is not the same as, has no identity with, the previous one in its line*; the aggregations that make up its composition being different from, having no identity with, those that made up the being of its predecessor. And yet it is not an entirely different being, since it is the same stream of Kamma-energy—though modified perchance by having shown itself in that last manifestation—which now is making its presence known in the sense-perceptible world as the new being. Thus we see, according to Buddhism, there is nothing that passes from one life to another *for there is nothing to pass*. The cessation of the *Khandhas* (Groups) in one life gives birth to some other *Khandhas* in another.'[2]

But this does not really explain *how* it takes place, or whether it is *thinkable* that it takes place, and the ancient mystery remains.

Though the overwhelming majority of Buddhists, in all periods and lands, have accepted this doctrine as an Article of Faith, its mystery has not greatly troubled them, because they have been content with the Hindu doctrine of Karma and Transmigration as a working theory of life, and this has saved Buddhism from moral chaos. The ordinary

[1] Mrs. Rhys Davids, *Buddhism*, p. 146.
[2] See *The Buddhist Chronicle*, March 12, 1922, p. 7.

Buddhist believes quite sincerely that he, in his own proper person, will live again to enjoy and suffer the rewards and penalties due to him from his present and former lives.

Buddhists usually ignore the teaching of their religion that in the next life, personal identity and memory will be lost. I never met, or heard of, a Buddhist in Ceylon who did not believe that his merit was so much greater than his demerit that he would be born into a higher and happier state of existence in the next life. Moreover, they believe that their dying thought will greatly influence their next birth (and the Pitakas support them in this). If, in their dying moment, they can suffuse their mind with happy, blissful thoughts, their good Karma will prevail over their evil Karma in the next existence. Their evil Karma will have its way with them eventually; it cannot be for ever evaded, but, by this device, the evil day may be postponed indefinitely.[1]

[1] See Sankhar-Uppatti Sutta, in the *Majjhima-Nikaya*, *S.B.B.*, Vol. VI, pp. 211-14.

XI

THE BUDDHA'S WAY OF SALVATION

Nirvana : What it is, and
How it is to be Attained

WHAT GOTAMA set out to find was *not* Nirvana, but *deliverance from Sorrow*. If we bear this in mind it will save us from many pitfalls in our thinking. Nirvana is a *negative*, and not a positive conception—it is nothing less than a *State of Sorrowlessness*.

The Buddha is represented as saying, in the *Samyutta-Nikaya* ' Sorrow alone arises where anything arises ; sorrow passes away where anything passes away.' No more comprehensive saying about sorrow could be imagined. And again we read in the *Cullavagga*, ' As the great sea, O disciples, is permeated by only one taste, the taste of salt, so also, O disciples, this Doctrine and this Law are pervaded by but one taste, *the taste of deliverance*.'

The message of the first Buddhist preachers was : ' Open ye your ears ; " *the deliverance from death is found*." ' Which, of course, meant also, *the deliverance from rebirth*. Gotama Buddha professed to have come into this world to show gods and men the way out of this sorrowful prison of *being*, with its gruesome attendants—birth, disease, old age, death, rebirth—into the freedom of *the cessation* of becoming, that is to say, Nirvana.

But the cause of ' becoming ' (rebirth) is desire, that clinging to existence which depends upon the illusion of individuality, i.e. ignorance. When ignorance is banished by enlightenment (knowledge), as the darkness vanishes before the light, existence, as the Buddha says, ' is cut off at the root; is made like a palm-tree stump, so that it can never more sprout again; can never more unfold itself.' In other words, with the cutting off of ignorance, the first link in the chain of cause and effect—of the series which ends in rebirth—is broken, and with it the whole series comes to an end. The man who perceives that the *self* he took to be *real* was only a shadow, a phantasm of the mind, has the assurance in his own heart ' This is my last existence; when death comes it is the end of all.' *That man has attained Nirvana.*

The price to be paid is a very high one—indeed the highest conceivable—being nothing less than his soul, his very self; but he pays it gladly and is content. The age-long struggle for existence now is over, the struggle that has involved him in ceaseless pain and sorrow. And with the ending of that struggle comes the cessation of desire, sorrowlessness, rich peace, quietness, contentment, ineffable restfulness, and bliss.

Such is the picture of Nirvana that we find portrayed in the early books. It is evident, therefore, that Nirvana was conceived of as something to be experienced and enjoyed *here and now*. The man who has attained Nirvana, no longer belongs to this world; he is not an actor in it, but a mere spectator, a looker-on. He finds in life nothing to desire or cling to. As we read in the *Dhammapada* 28 : ' The wise climbing the terraced heights of wisdom, looks down upon the fools : serene he looks upon the toiling crowd, as one who stands upon a mountain looks down upon those who stand upon the plain.'

Existence ending in Nirvana is conceived of as being something like that tree which blossoms only once, at the end of a hundred years, and then dies. The Buddha believed that countless existences come and go, but that at last an existence blossoms into saintship, perfection, and then passes away for ever.

In *Majjhima-N.* III 264–66, we have the account of the

venerable Channa's suicide. Channa fell sick and was in
great pain and dangerously ill. Sariputta, one of the greatest
of the Buddha's disciples, went with another, Mahā-Cunda,
to visit Channa, and they offered sympathy and help.
Channa replied that he had everything he needed, food, and
medicine, and attendance. 'But,' said he, 'I am losing
ground; my pains grow on me. I shall use the knife on
myself; I have no wish to live.' Sariputta tried to dissuade
him from this, and inquired whether, after his long service
of the Buddha, he was still enslaved by the senses. But
Channa replied that, on the contrary, he desired only *the
cessation of the elements of being.*

Then Sariputta said to him: 'You must think too,
Channa, of the Lord's eternal teaching that agitation marks
the enthralled; that the un-enthralled know no agitation;
that, if there be no agitation, there is serenity; that with
serenity there is no craving; that without craving there is
no round of rebirths; that without the round of rebirths
there is no passing hence, no arising elsewhere; that
without any passing hence or arising elsewhere there is no
further term in this world or elsewhere or both; and that
thus alone is Ill (*Dukkha*) ended for ever.'

Sariputta and Mahā-Cunda now left him, and, soon after
they had gone, Channa used the knife on himself. They
were greatly troubled at this, and took the news to the
Buddha, asking him what fate awaited Channa, and what his
destiny would be.

The Buddha replied that if a man 'divests' himself of
this body because he wants another body, he is blameworthy.
But that Channa did not desire another body (continuance
of existence), therefore he 'was blameless in using the knife
upon himself.'

'Thus spoke the Lord. Glad at heart, the reverend
Sariputta rejoiced in what the Lord had said.'[1]

[1] *S.B.B.*, Vol. VI, pp. 305-7.

To many writers on Buddhism it has appeared impossible that men and women should hail Nirvana, conceived of as being 'the cessation of becoming,' as ineffable bliss, joy unspeakable. This lack of understanding is due to a lack of sympathy with the Buddhist, and an inability to see the subject from the Buddhist's standpoint. To the believer in God, who conceives this life to be the one and only life, and believes that eternity lies before him with its infinite possibilities, the thought of extinction is intolerable.

The Buddhist, however, believes that he has lived from eternity, and that behind him lie millions of existences passed in earth, and heavens, and hells. The possibility of bringing this long and toilsome journey to an end, of escaping from 'the wheel of life,' on which he has been whirling since time began, gives him a sense of satisfaction, exaltation, and peace, which words cannot express. The certainty that this is his last existence brings to him exquisite happiness. He enjoys this wonderful experience now, and when the body dies he will have reached *Parinirvana*—dreamless peace.

Dr. Paul Dahlke, himself a very devout Buddhist, in his last book (*Buddhism and its Place in the Mental Life of Mankind*) wrote enthusiastically about the 'Joy' of the Buddha's message to mankind.

He says: 'Nibbana (Nirvana) *means* extinguishing, and *is* extinguishing. It is nothing but that which the word expresses. . . . Extinguishing is a process such as one may observe in every expiring flame (p. 214). " Extinguishing " here means not " putting out," but " dying out," as a flame flickers out for lack of fuel.'

Dr. Dahlke goes on to say: 'Life springs wholly and entirely out of Ignorance. . . . Ignorance ceases, means, the sufficient reason of life ceases. The sufficient reason of life ceases, means, life ceases' (p. 217). 'This is the joyful message, the gospel which the Buddha has to proclaim to men. To the actual thinker it is really a strange evangel when someone comes and says : " I declare to you eternal life." Of eternal life, beings assuredly will not fail ! What I call a joyful message is when one comes and says : " Behold, I show you the path upon which you can win free from eternal life ! " This path of escape the Buddha points out ; but he points it out only for him to whom life has become wholly and entirely suffering. " As of old, so also now I proclaim but one thing : Suffering and the Ceasing of Suffering ! " ' (p. 224).

Only to him who has come to regard existence in every conceivable world as ' wholly and entirely suffering,' can the message of the Buddha appear as a gospel, a joyful message.

What are we to understand *Parinirvana* to be ? What happens at death to the person who enjoys Nirvana in this life ? Does he sink into a trance-like sleep and remain in a state of unconscious existence for ever ? Some modern writers desire to hold this view, but they can find no confirmation of it in the ancient Buddhist writings, and it is contrary to the general trend and spirit of the Buddha's teaching. Whether the Buddha would, or would not, live on somewhere after the death of the body was a question which continued to agitate Gotama's disciples. Often did they put this question to him, but he invariably refused to give them a plain answer to their question.[1]

He did, however, on one occasion, give an answer which is very illuminating. It is recorded in the *Brahmajala* Sutta of the *Digha-Nikaya*, and is as follows :

' The outward form, brethren, of him who has won the truth (Tathagata), stands before you, but that which binds him to rebirth (viz : *tanha*, thirst) is cut in twain. So long as his body shall last, so long do gods and men behold him.

[1] For a striking example of this refusal, see *Cula Malunkya-Sutta, S.B.B.,* Vol. V, pp. 304-7.

On the dissolution of the body, beyond the end of his life, *neither gods nor men shall see him*.'[1]

Perhaps the nearest that he ever came to an explanation is contained in the following words : ' There is, disciples, a condition, where there is neither earth nor water, neither air nor light, neither limitless space, nor limitless time, neither any kind of being, neither ideation nor non-ideation, neither this world nor that world. There is neither *arising* nor *passing-away*, nor dying, neither cause nor effect, neither change nor standing-still.' That is *Parinirvana*, and what is it but the absolute cessation of all that we can think of as existence. This is what the majority of intelligent Buddhists believe, and there is little doubt that it is the right view.

The Buddha taught plainly and clearly that there is no ' *being* in this world or in any other world ; nothing that could abide, but only a *process of becoming.*' In view of this consistent teaching, it is inconceivable that he could have looked forward to any kind of existence after death—it would have been a denial of his whole philosophy. In dealing with the subject of Nirvana, it is difficult to find words which will not give a wrong impression and mislead the reader. We must not speak of extinction, for that would suggest ' *a real being*' which could become extinct. But the Buddha assures us again and again that there is no ' *real being*' at all, but only a ' *process*,' a ' *becoming*.' Therefore nothing is destroyed at death ; there is ' *a cessation of becoming*' and that is all.

That element in the man, which would have caused rebirth, renewed existence, is there no longer—he is like a lamp in which the oil is exhausted, and the light flickers out. In the Pitakas, the Buddha is reported to have said that at his death the *perfected saint* became extinct, like the flame of an expiring fire, whereof no man could say, the fire had gone out, went here, or went there. But *fire*, to the

[1] *S.B.B.*, Vol. II, p. 54.

Buddha, was the most perfect emblem of transiency, unreality, evanescence. As a Buddhist writer has said, ' *Parinirvana* is best conceived of in the terms of mathematics as *remainderlessness.*'

We have seen that the aim of both theoretical and practical Buddhism is to bring about the gradual quietening of the *elements of being*, and in the end, their extinction.

The elements of being in the ordinary man are conceived of as being perpetually in a state of commotion and turmoil.[1]

The visible signs of this internal commotion are greed, lust, envy, grasping, and all the other passions of the worldly man, and especially the desire for continued existence which arises out of the belief that he is a *person.* This state of tumult and unrest is the result of *ignorance.* When *wisdom* is attained all the elements in the stream of the individual existence come under its control. First of all, ' Wisdom perceives that there is no permanent personality (*pudgala, atma*), but that the supposed personality consists of the eighteen *dhatus.* As soon as this is perceived the " Path " is entered, and the end of the " Path " is in sight.' (See pp. 73–74.)

The perception that what he believed to be the *self*, is really *not-self* (*anatta*), leads to an immediate and profound change in the *elements of being* which make up the man ; their tumult is assuaged. Wisdom picks out the *elements* one by one, and thoroughly understands them—their causes and how they may be suppressed.

Now it has been proved by actual experiment that when a certain degree of intense concentration is reached, the sensations of taste and smell disappear, and it is assumed that the objects of these sensations, the matter, or the sense-data, of taste and odour, have likewise vanished. (See pp. 71–72.) On this foundation is built up a theory that all the sensations and sense-data can be eliminated ; that is to say

[1] See p. 97, ' Sariputta on cessation.'

they can be picked out one by one and suppressed, so that they can never return, ' and where before there was an *element*, now there is only a *blank* : this blank (*Nirodha*) is called " cessation through wisdom." '

But the number of *elements* which can be suppressed and eliminated by this method is very limited. Buddhists, however, believe in the existence of worlds into which men can be reborn, where there is no *sense-data* and where living beings have no *sense-consciousness*. In them the *dhatus* 1–5, 7–11, and 13–17 have disappeared, leaving blanks in their places, and nothing is left but pure consciousness, and non-sensuous objects. (See p. 74.)

They believe it possible, however, for the saint to obtain the same results—the suppression of *sense-consciousness*, and *sense-data*—in this life through ecstatic trances, called *Jhanas*.[1]

The *Jhanas*, when constantly practised, take on a more subtle and sublimated character.

Silacara Bhikkhu, in his book *The Noble Eightfold Path* (published in 1915), writes very clearly on this subject. On pages 164–65 he says : ' In the first of this set of specially refined states of consciousness, all idea of the existence of objects in a state of separation is lost, all discrimination between " a this " and " a that " is done away ; and there remains only a consciousness of an infinitude of space.

' In the next more refined state, the idea of infinite space is transcended, and its place taken by the idea of an infinitude of consciousness.

' In the next higher state, the idea of anything at all, of any kind of infinitude, whether of space or of consciousness, falls away, and the only idea present is that of nothingness.

' And in the last of these four higher, more sublimated *Jhanas*, all idea whatsoever ceases, whether of something or nothing. There is here neither perceiving nor yet not

[1] See the *Anguttara-Nikaya*, III, 88, translated by Warren, p. 288.

perceiving of aught; all predication, or possibility of predication, has come to utter end.'

It is enough now to say that, in the trances, the saint
reaches the realm where 'form' has ceased, and even
'space' has ceased. He passes into the realm of *nothingness*,
and beyond that into a realm where even *the consciousness of
nothingness* has ceased—into absolute negation. This con-
vinces him that all the *elements of being*, even *consciousness*, may
be suppressed and brought to utter end, so that where the
being made up of the eighteen *dhatus* stood, there will be
nothing.

We have already dealt with 'Consciousness' at some
length (see pp. 74, 80, 81, 86, 87, 91, 92, 93), but it is now
necessary to return to this subject, and consider it in
relation to Nirvana. As we read the Buddhist books we see
'consciousness' hovering about like the ghost of a soul,
and a very troublesome ghost it is.

On p. 86, we quoted the Buddha's words to Ananda:

> 'Were *vinnana* (consciousness), Ananda, not to
> descend into the mother's womb, would body and
> mind become constituted therein?'
> The answer is, 'No, they would not.'

We saw that the bhikkhu, Sati, believed that it was the
Buddha's own teaching that, 'It is *vinnana* which persists
and is reborn unchanged' (p. 87) and that the Buddha
denied that he had ever taught such a doctrine, and that the
bhikkhus confirmed him in this.[1]

But in the *Chain of Causality* we have this proposition,
'*From consciousness comes name and form*,' which seems to
point to *consciousness* as the link which connects the old with
the new being in the *karmic series*. This is confirmed by
Nagasena (see pp. 87–88) when he explains Rebirth without

[1] See *Majjhima-N.*, Maha-Tanha-Sankhya-Sutta, *S.B.B.*, Vol. V, pp. 183-91
for what is, probably, the Buddha's clearest teaching on 'Consciousness.'

Transmigration as like a lamp being lighted from another lamp : that is to say, the last flickering consciousness of the dying man lights a fresh consciousness in the new embryo. This comes perilously near to *the descent* of consciousness into the womb (p. 86), but Nagasena would have repudiated this view.

Now we will turn again to Buddhaghosa's attempt to explain Rebirth without Transmigration (pp. 91–92). He says that ' while the last conscious act (of the dying man) dies away, another conscious act arises in a new life, and this is called " rebirth " or " conception." ' We see here a real connexion between the *consciousness* of the dying man, and the consciousness which arises in the new embryo. But Buddhaghosa is careful to tell us that there is no actual contact—*the dying consciousness* does not alight on the new embryo, but disappears (in mid-stream) and a new consciousness arises.

Buddhism consistently teaches that nothing passes from the dying man to the new embryo except *Karma*. (And this is not contradicted by the saying, ' Nothing that is anything passes.') If it were proved that *consciousness passes over*, then some *thing* would pass, and the theory of Transmigration would be established—transmigration of *consciousness*—and it would be very difficult to distinguish this consciousness from a *soul*. We saw that Sati regarded ' the *vinnana* which persists and is reborn after death unchanged,' as ' that speaker, that feeler, who experiences the result of good and evil deeds done here or there.' This was indistinguishable from the Hindu conception of a ' soul that transmigrates.'[1]

We see, then, that the ' soul theory ' was always hovering about Buddhism, and endeavouring to creep in under the cloak of *consciousness*. Therefore, while it is true to say that

[1] See Mrs. Rhys Davids in *Sakya*, p. 158, also *Majjhima*, No. 38, and *Samyutta*, i, p. 122, iii, p. 106.

Rebirth is brought about by the force of Karma, it is equally true that without *consciousness* there could be no *new life* in the *karmic-series*, and that the new consciousness arises out of the dying consciousness, in some way that has never been satisfactorily explained. *Consciousness* forms a connecting link between the old and the new existence in every *series*, until a life blossoms into saintship. Then, the *karmic-force* having become spent, rebirth is at an end, and the consciousness of the dying perfect one vanishes into nothing, as the flame of the lamp flickers out when all the oil is exhausted; 'the consciousness has sunk to its rest.'

This is set forth in the story of the death of Channa, given above (p. 97). But even more clearly is 'the cessation of consciousness' illustrated in the story of the death of Godhika. Six times had Godhika 'touched temporary emancipation of mind, and then fell away therefrom.' The reason for his failure to reach *complete* emancipation is said to have been an internal ailment, which prevented prolonged concentration of mind. Despairing of success, Godhika thought within himself, 'What if I now use the knife?' (The idiom for this form of suicide). Mara, the evil one, who is hovering about intent on mischief, perceives with his mind Godhika's thought, and hastens into the Buddha's presence, and tells him that his follower is about to die without having *attained the final goal*.

But just then the venerable Godhika laid hands upon the knife. Then the Exalted One, discerning that this was Mara the evil one who spoke, addressed him in a verse:

> Ay, thus the strong in mind do go to work,
> No longing have they after living on,
> Craving and root of craving tearing out,
> *Hath Godhika passed utterly away.*

And the Exalted One addressed the brethren: 'Let us go, bhikkhus, to Black Rock on the slope of Seers' Hill,

where Godhika of the clansmen hath taken his own life.'
'Yea, lord,' said the brethren assenting. So they went
thither. And the Exalted One saw the venerable Godhika
afar lying (supine) on his couch with his shoulders twisted
round.

But just then a smokiness, a murkiness was going toward
the east, was going toward the west, was going toward the
north, was going toward the south, was going aloft, was
going downward, was going toward intervening points.

Then the Exalted One admonished the brethren : ' Do
ye not see, bhikkhus, that smokiness, that murkiness going
east, west, north, south, aloft, downward, and in between ? '

' Yes, lord.'

' That, bhikkhus, is Mara the evil one, who is seeking
everywhere for the consciousness of Godhika of the clansmen.

' Where,' he is thinking, ' hath Godhika's consciousness
been reinstated ? But Godhika of the clansmen, bhikkhus,
with a consciousness not reinstated hath utterly ceased to live.'

We see, therefore, that at the death of the saint, consciousness and all mental processes are extinguished, or
cease to be. Therefore, we must exclude from our idea of
Nirvana all feeling, volition, memory, and even consciousness.

Nirvana has been described as sorrowlessness, peace,
contentment, ineffable bliss. But these terms can be fittingly
applied only to the Nirvana of the living saint. They cannot
be used of the *Parinirvana* of the saint who has ' passed
utterly away,' like the Buddha or Godhika, except in the
sense that these saints have finally escaped from existence
altogether. Some Buddhists probably do regard this as
' ineffable bliss.'

Finally, we may say that whatever Nirvana may be conceived to be, it is at least *inanimate*.[1]

[1] See *The C.C. of Buddhism*, pp. 48-54.

I had intended to write a chapter on 'The Way to Nirvana Practically Considered,' but our limited space will not permit this. (Those who are interested in this aspect of Buddhism will find it described at some length in my *Ethics of Gotama Buddha*.) I can add here only a short note. ·

We have considered the Buddha's Way to Nirvana on its philosophical and technical side. But Gotama Buddha was not only a philosopher, he was also a practical teacher of ethics, and he taught the common people simple morality— rules concerning everyday life and conduct. This he regarded as the first rung in the ladder which leads to *the highest* (Nirvana) and every man must begin with this.

The next step was *renunciation*—the going forth from 'Home' to 'Homelessness.' This stage is characterized by self-concentration, which involves profound meditation supplemented by the '*Jhanas*.' (See pp. 102–103.)

The last step was the *attainment of wisdom*, when knowledge of the *non-ego*, and of the impermanence of all things, was personally realized, because this is a very personal matter, and each man must attain Nirvana by his own efforts, without the help of man or god. (See pp. 10, 11, 53.)

' Are three groups included in the Noble Eightfold Path, or is the Path included in the groups ?

' They are not included in it ; it is included in them. Right speech, right action, and right means of livelihood are included in the virtue-group ; right effort, right mindfulness, and right rapture of concentration are included in the concentration group ; while right outlook and right aims are included in the knowledge-group.'[1]

[1] *S.B.B.*, Vol. V, p. 215.

PART III

XII

THE ORDER OF THE BUDDHA'S DISCIPLES

To DESCRIBE 'The Order' in any adequate way would require a book at least as large as this. All that we can attempt here is to mention the chief points, and refer the reader to large books for fuller information.

The Buddha himself founded the Order, and formulated the laws by which it is controlled. These laws are set forth in the *Patimokkha*, which the student should read. It would be a mistake, however, to suppose that the Buddha started out with a perfect code of laws. To begin with there were only a few simple regulations, and he added to these from time to time as the need arose. In theory, all the laws which control the Order to this day were framed by the Buddha himself during his lifetime.[1] But in actual practice new laws and regulations were added. The sacred texts, however, show these too as issuing from the Buddha.

So long as the Buddha lived he was the Master of the Order; his personal authority was supreme, his decision was final. After his death the monks survived as a monastic community. Oldenberg suggests[2] that the formula of the three refuges, which the new recruit pronounced on entering the Order; 'I take refuge in the Buddha, in the Doctrine, and in the Order,' originated after the Buddha's death. I think this conjecture is almost certainly true. No one would think of taking refuge in the Order so long as the Buddha was living in their midst. After he had passed away, leaving

---

[1] See *Cullavagga* XI, pp. 1-9.
[2] See *Buddha*, p. 338.

no one man as his successor, men would regard the Order as a whole as his representative in the world.

Nevertheless, it would be a mistake to think of the Order as a compact organization, like, for example, the Roman Catholic Church, which regards the Pope as Christ's representative on earth. There was no central authority in Buddhism, either individual or Church Court, to enforce the law and to maintain discipline. Even the decisions of the Council held at Rajagaha did not command universal assent, (see p. 22) and the Council had no means of enforcing its decision ; each community might accept as much or as little as it thought fit.

When the Buddha refused to appoint a successor to himself (see p. 53) he left his community like sheep without a shepherd, or like a rudderless ship upon the ocean. In the earliest days, schisms arose within the Order ; dissensions and discords which bore in themselves the germs of dissolution. Lack of central organization was, probably, chiefly responsible for the ultimate disappearance of Buddhism from India, the land of its birth.

Entry into the Order was, in theory, open to any one, inasmuch as every one was subject to suffering and rebirth. In actual life, however, certain restrictions on admission to the Order had to be imposed. For example :

(1) Those could not be admitted who were suffering from certain diseases and sicknesses, such as consumption, leprosy, epilepsy.
(2) Nor confirmed criminals.
(3) Nor persons in the Royal Service, such as soldiers.
(4) Nor debtors and slaves.
(5) Nor sons without their parents' consent.
(6) Nor persons under 20 years of age.

The ceremony of initiation is completed in two grades : (1) there is the preparatory ordination, *Pabbajja*, i.e. *the outgoing* from 'home' to 'homelessness,' or from some other monastic sect, (2) the *Upasampada*, i.e. *the arrival*, which is the entry into the circle of the bhikkhus. He does not belong to the Order until he has received this higher initiation. We have not space to describe the *Upasampada* ceremony,[1] but can only mention the four great prohibitions.

(1) An ordained monk may not have sexual intercourse, not even with an animal.
(2) He may not take what has not been given him, what is called theft—not even a blade of grass.
(3) He may not knowingly deprive any creature of life, not even a worm or an ant.
(4) He may not boast of any superhuman perfection.

He who keeps the vows expressed in this confession has reached the grade of *Sotapanna* on *the path*, the lowest class of those who have attained *the path*. These are not liable to rebirth in the lower worlds (hells, spirit-worlds, and worlds of lower animals); they are sure of deliverance; they shall eventually attain the highest knowledge.[2]

The communication of these four prohibitions concludes the ceremony of ordination. This ordination does not bind for life; at any time, and for any reason, the monk may retire from the Order, and return to the home life. The ordained monk must also observe the ten duties, sometimes called the ten commandments. (*Dasa-sila*.) (1) To abstain from killing, (2) theft, (3) falsehood, (4) sexual intercourse, (5) intoxicants, (6) eating after midday, (7) from dancing, singing, drum-beating, witnessing ludicrous exhibitions, (8) from indulging in perfumes, unguents, personal adornments, &c., (9) from the use of high and luxurious seats or beds, (10) from accepting gold, or silver, or money.

[1] See Oldenberg's *Buddha*, pp. 345-52. See also Warren, pp. 395-410 for a detailed account of an ordination service performed in Kandy, Ceylon.
[2] *Mahaparinibbana-Sutta*; see also pp. 51-52 of this book.

E

The monk takes upon himself the vow of poverty. Property was felt to be a fetter upon the spirit struggling for freedom. As an individual he may possess the following articles : (1) a set of three garments (to be worn together), (2) a girdle for the loins, (3) an alms-bowl, (4) a razor, (5) a needle, (6) a water-strainer. As a community the monks may possess many other things, including books, houses and lands, and much else.

During the first five years after ordination the monk is required to place himself under the guidance and instruction of two able monks, who shall have belonged for at least ten years to the Order. These are his teachers, and he must give them service and obedience.

There was nothing in the way of differences of rank in the Order, except those which belonged to greater seniority —reckoned from the date of ordination.

Physical labour of any kind was always foreign to this monastic life—not even gardening was allowed. The whole life and all the energies were claimed for religious exercises.

Twice in the month, at full moon and at new moon, the monks of each district, wherever they might happen to be sojourning, came together to celebrate the abstinence day. (Now they gather four times a month, according to the phases of the moon, called in Ceylon *poya* days.) The most important element in these meetings was the confessional celebration. No monk was allowed to absent himself, unless he was too ill to be moved : if possible, he was to be brought to the assembly on his sick bed.

The ceremony begins with the enumeration of the *four sins* (p. 113), which involve expulsion from the Order. If any one of the monks has been guilty of any of these sins, he is exhorted to confess his fault without any evasion or holding back. Then follows investigation into lesser sins. (At a later date it was ordained that confession must be made in private to a senior monk before coming into the assembly.) There was no idea of the Buddha being spiritually in their midst, as Christ is believed to be present when His followers are gathered in His name. He has attained Nirvana.

There was also an annual ceremony for the monks at the close of the rainy season (*Vassa* or *Was*) called the ceremony of *invitation* (*Pavarana*), when all the monks of the district came together and invited their brethren to name any faults they had observed in one another during the period of retirement. (See p. 44.)

These few ceremonious observances took the place, for the monks, of regular acts of public worship. For the rest, each monk must work out his *own* salvation : no man or god could help or hinder him in this.[1]

A few words must be added about the Order of nuns, though this could never compare in importance with the Order of monks, and in modern times in most Buddhist countries it has practically ceased to exist.[2]

The Buddha himself was strongly opposed to the proposal to admit women to the Order. Women are, to the Buddhist, of all the snares which the tempter has spread for men the most dangerous ; in women are embodied all the powers of infatuation, which bind the mind to the world. On one occasion Ananda, who could never rid himself of the high regard for women which he had conceived in his youth, inquired from the Buddha, ' Master, how shall we behave before women ? ' ' You should shun their gaze, Ananda.' ' But if we see them, master, what then are we to do ? ' ' Not speak to them, Ananda.' ' But if we do speak to them, master, what then ? ' ' Then you must keep wide awake, Ananda.'

[1] See ' Introduction,' pp. 10, 11, 53, and 56.
[2] Attempts have been made during recent times in Ceylon to revive the Order of nuns, but with little success.

Our limited space will not allow us to give, even in outline, the interesting story of the founding of the Order of nuns. (See Warren, pp. 441–47.) We must confine ourselves to the essentials of the Order. It was with the gravest misgivings, and against his better judgement, that the Buddha at last yielded to the pressure of his foster-mother, Mahapajapati (see p. 28), to receive women as his disciples. He told Ananda, at the time, that this act would result in serious loss to his religion, and to its final overthrow.

The Buddha took the precaution of placing the Order of nuns (*Bhikkhuni-Sangha*) under the guardianship of the Order of monks (*Bhikkhu-Sangha*). This subordination is seen in the following rules, and many others :

(1) A nun, if she have been ordained even a hundred years ago, must bow most reverently before every monk, even though he be ordained only this day, rise in his presence, raise her clasped hands, duly honour him.
(2) Under no circumstances is a nun to revile or scold a monk.
(3) From this day forward is the path of speech (by way of accusation) against the monks closed to the nuns. Yet is not the path of speech against the nuns closed to the monks.

Yet, in spite of all this, the Buddha found amongst women some of his most devoted disciples and most generous supporters, and the same is true today.

THE ORDER OF LAYMEN

The Buddha's Community is a community of monks and nuns. Only those who have given up everything can be the Buddha's real disciples. But surrounding this inner circle of the elect was an outer circle of lay-devotees, men and women (*upasaka* and *upasika*). It is clear that an Order of mendicants could not be thought of apart from a laity prepared to support them by works of beneficence. Some of these were received by the recital of a definite formula, 'I take my refuge with the Exalted One, and with the Doctrine, and with the Order of the disciples. May the Exalted One accept me as his *upasaka* from this day forward through my life, me who have taken refuge with him.'

The *upasaka* was not necessarily, however, like the *bhikkhu*, separated from other teachers and sects, and entirely devoted to the Buddha ; he might at the same time be the *upasaka* of another sect. It also appears that many generous supporters of the Buddha and his Order, who had not formally taken refuge with him, were called upasakas, for it is said, ' In truth he is an upasaka who shows himself to be so by his acts.'

Devout laymen and women vow to keep the first five or eight (*pansil* or *atasil*) of the ten commandments for shorter or longer periods of time. Some renew the vow on every moon-day (*poya* day)—four times a month. This is called ' taking *Sil*.' Some take the vow for twenty-four, thirty-six, or forty-eight hours, and remain at the temple until it is fulfilled, because they cannot hope to keep the commandments at home, under the conditions of their ordinary life. (See p. 57.)

A few give up the home life, without becoming monks or nuns, and become itinerating mendicants. These have a better chance of keeping their vows, as all their needs are supplied by others, and they are removed from the temptations of ordinary life.

No regular religious gatherings were instituted for the laity, and much less were they permitted to join the monks in their general assemblies. By the daily begging-round the monks kept in touch with the laity, and so had opportunities of giving them religious help in times of trouble or sickness. (See p. 44.)

By deeds of beneficence to the Buddha and his Order

the laity were able to heap up merit for themselves, and were assured of great rewards. ' Well is it for a man always to dispense boiled rice if he have a desire for joy, whether he seek heavenly joy or long for earthly happiness.'[1]

How to acquire merit has been reduced in Ceylon to an exact science. Merit may be obtained in many ways, as, for example, by living a good life and cultivating character, but this is a slow process, and its yield in merit is very disappointing. A much more profitable method is by alms-giving, as the following precepts will show.

' Feed a cow or a dog, and you will have long life, prosperity, beauty, power, and wisdom in a hundred births.'

' Feed a man who does not keep the precepts, and you will have these benefits in a thousand births. Feed one who keeps the precepts and you will enjoy them in a myriad births.'

' He who offers food, or a flower, to the Buddha, will reap more merit than if he had fed all the inhabitants of the world. That the Buddha is extinct is of no consequence, as he is fully represented by the Bo-tree, the relics, or the image.'

' The offering of food to a holy priest is itself more profitable than feeding all the beggars in the world.'

We see to what extravagant proportions this teaching about the merit of alms-giving has grown.

[1] *Mahavagga* VI, 24, 6. See also *Majjhima-Nikaya*, 135, *Sutta Sangaha*, 6, and *Cullavagga*, VI.

XIII

THE HISTORICAL DEVELOPMENT OF BUDDHISM

WE HAVE already pointed out (pp. 43–44) that the Buddha's own wanderings were confined to the kingdoms of Kosala and Magadha, and the free States around them. For some centuries after his death the influence of Buddhism slowly and gradually widened in India. It was regarded rather as a sect of Brahmanism than as a new religion. During this period its troubles were within, rather than without, in the growing dissensions and divisions of the Order. (See p. 112.)

In an earlier part of this book we referred to the Councils held from time to time to settle disputed points of doctrine and discipline. (See pp. 17–18.) The history of these Councils has been preserved in the *Cullavagga*.

By the time the second Council was held, the Buddhists were already split up into eighteen different sects belonging to the four schools of thought called *Mahasanghika, Sthavira, Sarvastivada*, and *Sammitiya*.

In the second century of its existence, Buddhism, like all else in India, was greatly influenced by the appearance of Alexander the Great on India's western frontier, and it was probably this which led to the formation of the great united North Indian Kingdom under Chandragupta.

Chandragupta and his son Bindusara, were not Buddhists, but rather favoured the Brahmans. His grandson King Asoka, however, became the greatest Buddhist missionary of history. It was under his patronage that Buddhism became the paramount religion of India, and was carried to Ceylon, and during the next thousand years to Burma, Siam, Cambodia, Annam, Tibet, China, Mongolia, Korea and Japan, Java, and other countries. We cannot trace in any adequate way the history of this development in one short chapter, but the reader is referred especially to *Buddhism as a Religion* by H. Hackmann, pp. 36–92, where he will find this admirably done.

Asoka is also famous for the large number of inscriptions on pillars and rock-walls, which he left behind. These deal chiefly with the moral precepts and social rules of Buddhism. There is an excellent little book on Asoka in *The Hermitage of India* series, by J. M. Macphail, M.A., M.D., which may be consulted for detailed information.[1]

The large empire of Asoka fell to pieces soon after his death, and then followed an invasion by the Greeks, who exercised a great influence on Indian Culture. The most distinguished of the Greek Kings of this period was Menander (Milinda) about the second century B.C. He is *the king* in *The Questions of King Milinda*, and in that book we see the clash of Indian and Greek thought. (See pp. 77–78.)

Later on came the Scythian invasion, and the founding of the Indo-Scythian or Kushan Empire. The greatest of the Scythian Kings, Kanishka, adopted Buddhism, and called together a Council of Buddhist leaders at Jalandhara in Kashmir. We have no real knowledge of what happened at this Council, but it is evident that the great division of Buddhism into the *Mahayana* and *Hinayana* schools was made about this time. The great Mahayana teacher Asvaghosa also lived in the days of Kanishka.

In spite of this great cleft in the religion, or perhaps because of it, Buddhism seems to have enjoyed its greatest popularity and material prosperity in India during the next few hundred years. When the Chinese pilgrim Fa-hian visited India about A.D. 400 he found Buddhism flourishing

[1] See also V. A. Smith, *Asoka*.

in great strength and pomp, but it had been transformed into a popular religion, by the amalgamation of supernatural and magical elements which were foreign to the religion of its founder.[1] It was during this period that *Tantrism* arose in Buddhism with its strongly marked sexual character and immoral influence.

When in the seventh century another Chinese Pilgrim, Yuan Chuang (or Hiuen-Tsiang), visited India he found a Buddhism that was slowly decaying and falling to pieces : it had become a system of relic worship, miracles, magic, exorcism, nature worship, and much else that showed its degeneracy.[2] This inward decay continued its destruction until the eleventh century A.D., when the Muslim invasion of India swept away what remained of this degenerate Buddhism. Since then it has not existed as a religion in India, and Ceylon became the land to which men looked for Buddhism in its purity. Here the *Pali Tripitaka* was edited, and commentaries written on it, especially by Buddhaghosa.[3]

Buddhism was introduced into Ceylon from India, about 250 B.C., by Asoka's son Mahendra, or Mahinda. The tradition that Asoka's missionaries reached Burma is probably true. A purer form of Buddhism, however, was introduced from Ceylon perhaps as early as the seventh or eighth century (but certainly later than Buddhaghosa, fifth century A.D.), and this is the prevailing type to-day, though there are traces in Burma of an older, and more corrupt form of Buddhism.[4]

Buddhism was known in Cambodia in the seventh century (though it may have been introduced a century

---

[1] See *Buddhist Records of the Western World*, by Beal, p. xi, and Book III, p. 119, footnote.
[2] For details see *Life of Hiuen-Tsiang*, by Beal, and the footnote quoted above.
[3] See *Buddhaghosa*, by B. C. Law.
[4] *E.R.E.*, Vol. III, pp. 20, 38, 39.

or two earlier, see *E.R.E.* Vol. III, p. 156), and had become powerful by the ninth century. It has also been the national religion of Siam from the founding of the Siamese kingdom in the fourteenth century to the present day.

Buddhism entered Tibet not later than the seventh century, and the first monastery is said to have been built in the year A.D. 749.

Though legends state that Buddhism was introduced into China in the year 217 B.C., the real historical date is probably during the reign of the Emperor Ming-Ti (A.D. 58–76). Buddhism came to Korea from China in or about A.D. 372, Japan received Buddhism from Korea in about A.D. 522 or 534, but for a long time it made very slow progress.[1]

The Chinese Buddhist pilgrim, Fa-hian, found a very feeble Buddhism in Java in A.D. 412. It had become very vigorous, however, in the seventh century A.D., and continued to flourish alongside Saivism until both were overthrown by the Muhammadan invasion in the fifteenth century A.D. The history of Buddhism in Sumatra is very similar to that of Java, both in its rise and in its over-throw.[2]

In the Island of Bali, however, Buddhism still survives, to some extent, alongside a very ancient form of Brahmanism. In all these Islands (Java, Sumatra, Bali, &c.) it is probable that Buddhism was the religion of the King and the upper classes, and that Saivism prevailed more widely amongst the common people, but both religions left it open for the same individuals to be Buddhists and Saivites at the same time.[3]

[1] See *E.R.E.*, Vol. VII, pp. 482-83.
[2] ibid., pp. 495-97.
[3] For evidence of this see *E.R.E.* reference above.

XIV

BUDDHISM AS A RELIGION

We have space to deal with only two or three fundamental aspects of this subject, but the reader is recom-
mended to consult Hackmann's *Buddhism as a Religion*,
especially pp. 93–299, for detailed information.

Buddhism in its original form was not a religion for
the multitudes—only the elect few could receive and
practise it. A Buddhist writer, referring to the statement
that Buddhism is a ' gospel ' for the poor, says :

' I think that anything more untrue could scarcely be said,
for if there is anything which we can *not* say of Buddhism it is
this. The poor man, who has never yet tasted the joys of this
world, will scarcely grow enthusiastic over a renouncing of
every lust of life. An ideal state must be set before him in a
heaven that will make up to him two-fold for what was denied
him here below. The religion of the poor is a religion of
promises. The Buddhist religion, however, is a religion of
renunciation.'[1]

It is historically true that Gotama Buddha drew his
followers chiefly from the ranks of the Brahmans, nobles,
and wealthy merchant classes. (See pp. 39–40.)

How then are we to account for the fact that there are
said to be at least four hundred millions of Buddhists in the
world at the present day ?

The explanation is that Buddhism, wherever it has spread,
has tolerated, and in most cases adopted, the religion of the
people it was attempting to win.

[1] Dalke, *Essays*, pp. 59–61.

Even in India Buddhism made itself popular by transforming itself into a religion of magic and miracle. It invented gods and heavens without number; it set up images, and organized gorgeous processions, and these methods succeeded for a time. (See pp. 120–121.) But in the end it failed in competition with Brahmanism for the popular favour. Brahmanism had a religion for the common man with which Buddhism, in its most diluted state, could not compete.

A corrupt form of Buddhism was introduced into Tibet from India (see p. 122), where it allied itself with the dreadful superstitions and savage practices of the fierce and uncouth mountain people it found there. Their religion was called *Bon*, and it demanded, amongst other fearful things, human sacrifices. This religion became completely mixed up with *Tantric* Buddhism.[1]

Modern Buddhism in Tibet is called *Lamaism*, and it is one of the most bewildering polytheistic and idolatrous systems known to man.[2] It would be difficult to imagine a religion farther removed from the original teaching of the Buddha than this is; and it is not the insignificant element of Buddhism which makes this religion attractive to the common people, but the foreign elements imported into it. Buddhism occupies a more dominating position in Tibet than in any other part of the world.

The Buddhism of China and Japan, like that of Tibet, belongs to the *Mahayana* School, and in Mongolia and some parts of China *Lamaism* is the prevailing type. And here I would draw the attention of the reader to the fact that the majority of the four hundred millions of Buddhists said to be in the world today are to be found in these two countries. But every Chinese Buddhist is first of all a Confucianist or a Taoist (or both) and a Buddhist second; while almost every Japanese Buddhist is also a Shintoist. Hackmann

[1] See Hackmann, pp. 71-77.   [2] ibid., pp. 155-99.

says (p. 257) that the laity of China cannot rightly be considered a Buddhist people. 'In the statistics of Chinese religions, only the monks should be reckoned as Buddhists. The laity merely have to do with Buddhism as regards its externals, and share very little in its genuine ideas.'

Buddhism is not an exclusive religion like Christianity or Muhammadanism, it is quite ready to share the allegiance of any people with another religion, and this is one secret of its wide-spread influence.

When we turn to *Hinayana* Buddhism, we find that the original doctrines of the *Pali Pitakas* have been preserved in Ceylon, Burma, and Siam. Of these three, Ceylon has been most careful to keep the doctrine pure, though, as a religion, Buddhism is more influential in the daily life of Burma and Siam. But even in these lands, where, to the visitor, there appears to be so true a devotion to the Buddha, all the Buddhists have other religions to which they turn in time of trouble.

When Buddhism was introduced into Burma, the prevailing religion of the people was *Nat* worship—the worship of demons and nature spirits.[1] Buddhism absorbed this religion to such an extent that attempts are being made by present-day Buddhists to identify these *Nats* with certain figures of Buddhist mythology, namely, the *devas*, who inhabit the lower heavens. Even Buddhist monks are dominated by *Nat* worship to an almost incredible extent, and regular provision is made in the village monasteries for the comfort and well-being of the temple *Nat*.[2]

Ceylon is no exception to this rule. Here we find layer upon layer of different religious beliefs, with Buddhism covering the surface. The religion of the ordinary Sinhalese Buddhist now is much the same as that of his ancestors

---

[1] See *E.R.E.*, Vol. III, pp. 20, 21, 36, 47.
[2] Hackmann, pp. 147-51.

two thousand years ago. His mind is a strange mingling of conflicting and contradictory beliefs.

My space is so limited that I can do little more than name the religions of the Sinhalese Buddhist.

I. First there is *Kapuism*.

The temples of this religion are called *dewalas* and its priests *Kapuwas*. These temples are maintained and used by Buddhists, and their priests and priestesses are Buddhists. Some of these temples are dedicated to such well-known Hindu gods as *Karttikeya* (also called *Kandaswami, Kataragama deviyo,* &c.). *Dewalas* dedicated to this god are found in Kataragama, Dondra, Badulla, Kandy, and many other places in Ceylon. Near the Dalada Maligawa (The Temple of the Tooth) in Kandy stand the four great *dewalas* of *Natha, Maha Vishnu, Kataragama,* and *Pattiny*. These *dewalas* are closely associated with the Dalada Maligawa, especially in connexion with the *Perahera* ceremonies. There is a small *dewala* in the courtyard of nearly every Buddhist *vihara* in Ceylon, and, in some places, they are both found under the same roof, as, for example, at Lankatilaka near Kandy. Buddhists pass from the *vihara* to the *dewala*.

The worship of *Vishnu* is closely associated with Buddhism. Hindus believe the Buddha to be an *avatar*, or incarnation of *Vishnu*. Most Buddhist temples in Ceylon have a room set apart for the image of *Vishnu*, who is worshipped as a *deva*.

In many *dewalas* inferior gods (*dewatawo*) are worshipped and propitiated by particular ceremonies. Some of these gods are Hindu deities, others deified heroes of the Sinhalese. While Buddhism has to do chiefly with future lives, *Kapuism* has more to do with the interests of this world, and the help sought by its worshippers is more material than religious.

II. Next we have *Grahaism* (the worship of the gods of the planets).

This religion is built up on the theory that the gods of the planets control the lives of men. A horoscope is cast for every Buddhist child, and the influence of the astrologer, which begins at birth (or before), will only end with the person's death. The horoscope must be consulted before every important step in life. From it is found the lucky day for the young child to have its first meal of rice, the lucky day to begin school-life, and much besides.

' The horoscope of a man is the essential thing for determining both the nature of the planetary influence which troubles him at a particular time with disease or some other evil, and also the nature of the particular ceremony necessary to remedy the evil.'[1] The planet god, who is the cause of the evil, is propitiated by certain ceremonies called *Bali* ceremonies, which are too varied and intricate to be described in these notes.

III. *Demonism.*

The Demonism of Ceylon is much older than Buddhism and is the bedrock religion of the Sinhalese.[2] The demons worshipped are not the gentle and benevolent demons of the *Pali Pitakas*, but real devils, cruel and merciless, who form a large community under the government of a demon king called Wessamuny.

At one time these demons were free to seize men, and to ' swallow them down alive like so many oysters,' as a Sinhalese writer puts it. Later their liberty was curtailed by their king, and now they are only permitted to inflict

---

[1] See a paper on ' The Bali Ceremonies of the Sinhalese,' by W. A. de Silva, J.P., in the Journal of the Ceylon Branch of the Royal Asiatic Society, 1911.
[2] See *The Government of Ceylon Census Report of* 1911, pp. 260-61.

disease or death at the request of devil-priests who give them offerings, with which they must be content.

'In every demon ceremony, which is performed either to cure or inflict sickness, or to protect a person from becoming liable to any "demon sickness" at all, the effective agents, which influence the demons, and, through them, the disease, are Charms or Spells, Invocations, and *Dolla* or offering, especially the first, with or without the last two. The Charms, or *Mantra*, as they are called, are generally in Sanskrit, Tamil, or Sinhalese, but a few are written in other languages, such as Arabic, Persian, Telagu, Malayalim, Bengali, and others.

'Whatever be the nature of the disease brought on a man by *Hooniyan* charms, that disease always resists every attempt to cure it by medicine, and invariably results in the death of the man, unless other remedies are applied in time, namely those which charms alone afford.

'There is no power on earth or in the heavens, neither Buddhist ceremonies against demons (*pirit* and *piritnool*) nor the invocation of superior gods, which can save a man from the vengeance of demons after he has been devoted to them by charms, except superior charms of the same sort which are able to bind the demons and restrain them. This every Sinhalese Buddhist knows.'[1]

It is sometimes said that demon ceremonies are now performed in Ceylon only in interior districts amongst the most illiterate Buddhists. But this is not true. For example, in the village where I am now living, four miles out of Kandy, and only half a mile from the Kandy-Colombo main road, Devil Ceremonies are frequently performed.

The following Statistics, which are taken from the Ceylon Government Census of 1921 (the latest official figures available, but accepted by Buddhists as approximately

[1] See a paper on 'Devil Worship,' by D. de Silva Gooneratne Modliar in the Journal of the Ceylon Branch of the Royal Asiatic Society, 1865.

correct now in 1934) will give some idea of the prevalence of these cults.

Buddhist Monks			10,097
Devil Priests and Devil Dancers, and *Priests and Priestesses of Dewalas*	males 2,289 females 1,572		3,861
Astrologers (*Priests and Priestesses of the Planet gods*)	males 1,077 females 816		1,893

Thus briefly we have tried to give the reader a general idea of the Religious Beliefs of Buddhists, and especially of the Sinhalese Buddhist. While it is true that he professes Buddhism, and professes it sincerely, for practical purposes he associates it chiefly with joyous holidays, and festivals, and pilgrimages, which are, really, holiday excursions and opportunities for social intercourse. He finds little consolation for his present troubles in this religion—for such consolations he must look elsewhere.

APPENDIX I

LITERATURE

(This list contains only a few selected books, which the author has found especially useful, and which he recommends to students.)

I. THE BUDDHA AND HIS DOCTRINE

Author	*Title of Book and Publishers*
OLDENBERG, H. . .	*Buddhism*. Williams and Norgate, London, 1882.
RHYS DAVIDS, T. W. .	*Buddhism*. Society for Promoting Christian Knowledge, London, 1912.
Do.	*Buddhism, its History and Literature*. Putnam's Sons, Ltd., 1926.
Do.	*Hibbert Lectures*, 1881.
KEITH, A. BERRIEDALE .	*Buddhist Philosophy*. Oxford University Press, 1923.
COPLESTON, R. S. . .	*Buddhism, Primitive and Present*. Longmans, Green, and Co., 1892.
GOGERLY, D. J. . .	*Ceylon Buddhism*. 2 Vols., Kegan Paul, Trench, Trubner & Co., Ltd., 1908.
DAHLKE, PAUL . .	*Buddhist Essays*. Macmillan & Co., Limited, London, 1908.
Do.	*Buddhism, and its Place in the Mental Life of Mankind*. Macmillan & Co., Ltd., London, 1927.

Author	*Title of Book and Publishers*
GEDEN, A. S.	*Studies in Eastern Religions.* Charles H. Kelly, London, 1900.
Do.	*What is Buddhism? An answer from the Western Point of View.* Published by The Buddhist Lodge, London, 1928.
SILACARA, BHIKKHU	*The Four Noble Truths.* Theosophical Publishing House, Madras, 1922.
Do.	*The Noble Eightfold Path.* Theosophical Publishing House, Madras, 1922.
WARD, C. H. S.	*The Ethics of Gotama Buddha.* Colombo, 1923.
RHYS DAVIDS, C. A. F.	*Sakya, or Buddhist Origins.* Kegan Paul, Trench, Trubner & Co., Ltd., London, 1931.
Do.	*Gotama the Man.* Luzac & Co., London, 1928.
Do.	*A Manual of Buddhism.* The Sheldon Press, 1932.
Do.	*Buddhist Psychology.* The Quest Series, 1914.
Do.	*Buddhism.* Williams & Norgate, London.
STCHERBATSKY, TH.	*The Central Conception of Buddhism and the Meaning of the word 'Dharma.'* Royal Asiatic Society, 1923.
SADAW, LEDI	*Some Points in Buddhist Doctrine.* The Pali Text Society, London, 1914.
DEUSSEN, PAUL	*The Upanishads.* T. & T. Clark, 1906.
RADHAKRISHNAN, S.	*The Philosophy of the Upanishads.* George Allen & Unwin Ltd., 1924.

Author	Title of Book and Publishers
KEITH, A. B.	Samkhya System. Oxford University Press, London.

See also many valuable articles in Hastings' *Encyclopedia of Religion and Ethics.*

II. TRANSLATIONS FROM THE BUDDHIST *Canon* AND OTHER AUTHORITATIVE *Pali* BOOKS

RHYS DAVIDS, T. W.	*Dialogues of the Buddha* (translated from the *Pali* of the *Digha-Nikaya*), (*Sacred Books of the Buddhists*), Vol. II.
RHYS DAVIDS, T. W. and C. A. F.	*Dialogues of the Buddha* (translated from the *Pali* of the *Digha-Nikaya*), (*Sacred Books of the Buddhists*), Vols. III and IV.
CHALMERS, LORD	*Further Dialogues of the Buddha* (translated from the *Pali* of the *Majjhima-Nikaya*), Vols. V and VI.

The following are published by the Pali Text Society:

RHYS DAVIDS, C. A. F.	*Kindred Sayings* (*Samyutta-Nikaya*), Parts I, II, and III.
WOODWARD, F. L.	*Kindred Sayings* (*Samyutta-Nikaya*), Parts IV and V.
Do.	*Gradual Sayings* (*Anguttara-Nikaya*), Vols. I and II.
HARE, E. M.	*Gradual Sayings* (*Anguttara-Nikaya*), Vol. III.
RHYS, DAVIDS, C. A. F.	*Psalms of the Early Buddhists* (*Thera-therigatha*).
Do.	I. *Psalms of the Sisters.*
Do.	II. *Psalms of the Brethren.*

Author	*Title of Book and Publishers*
AUNG, S. Z. and RHYS DAVIDS, C. A. F.	*Points of Controversy*, being a translation of the *Katha-Vatthu* from the *Abhidhamma-Pitaka*.
Do.	*Compendium of Philosophy*, being a translation of the *Abhidhammattha-Sangaha*.
MAUNG TIN, P.	*The Path of Purity*, Vols. I, II, and III. (Being a translation of Buddhaghosa's *Visuddhimagga*.)
MAUNG TIN, P. and RHYS DAVIDS, C. A. F.	*The Expositor*, Buddhaghosa's *Atthasalini*. Vols. I and II.
GEIGER, W.	*The Mahavamsa, or the Great Chronicle of Ceylon*.
GEIGER, W.	*The Culavamsa*, being the more recent part of the *Mahavamsa*, Parts I and II.
RHYS DAVIDS, T. W.	*The Questions of King Milinda, Sacred Books of the East*, Vols. XXXV and XXXVI.
WARREN, H. C.	*Buddhism in Translations*. Published by Harvard University, 1909.
LAW, B. C.	*A History of Pali Literature*. Vols. I and II. Kegan Paul, 1933.
NARIMAN, G. K.	*Literary History of Sanskrit Buddhism*. (From Winternitz, Slyvain Levi, Huber.) Indian Book Depot, Bombay, 1923. (Invaluable for English students.)

For a complete list of English Translations of the *Pali Pitakas*, see *Sakya*, pp. 435–36.

III. MISCELLANEOUS LITERATURE

HACKMANN, H.	*Buddhism as a Religion*. Probsthain and Co., London, 1910. (Every student of Buddhism ought to read this book.)

Author	*Title of Book and Publishers*
BEAL, S.	*Buddhist Records of the Western World.* Kegan Paul.
Do.	*The Life of Hiuen-Tsiang.* Kegan Paul, 1914.
GORDON, E. A.	' *World-Healers,' or The Lotus Gospel and its Bodhisattvas.* Eugene L. Morice, 9 Cecil Court, Charing Cross Road, London.
RICHARD, T.	*The New Testament of Higher Buddhism.* T. & T. Clark, Edinburgh.
HARDY, R. S.	*A Manual of Buddhism.* Partridge & Oakley, London.
RHYS DAVIDS, T. W.	*Buddhist India.* T. Fisher Unwin, London, 1911.
RHYS DAVIDS, C. A. F.	*The Milinda-Questions.* George Routledge & Sons, London, 1930.
SILACARA BHIKKHU	*Lotus Blossoms.* Theosophical Publishing House, Adyar, Madras, 1922.
Do.	*The Five Precepts.* Theosophical Publishing House, Adyar, Madras, 1913.
BHIKKHU SUBHADRA	*The Message of Buddhism.* Kegan Paul, London, 1922.
LAW, B. C.	*Buddhaghosa.* Thacker, Spink & Co., Calcutta, 1923.
MACPHAIL, J. M.	*Asoka.* Oxford University Press, London.
STREETER, B. H.	*The Buddha and the Christ.* Macmillan & Co., London, 1932.
FARQUHAR, J. N.	*The Religious Literature of India.* Oxford University Press, 1920.
THOMAS, E. J.	*The History of Buddhist Thought.* Kegan Paul, London, 1933.

For a fuller list of Buddhist Literature, see Hackmann, *Buddhism as a Religion,* pp. 300–8.

APPENDIX II

INDEX OF NAMES

A

Aboriginals of North India, 84
Acchariya Manussa, 10
African Tribes, 83
Ajātasattu, 49
Ālāra of Kālāma, 35
Alexander the Great, 119
All-Soul, 68
Ambapali the Courtesan, 42, 46, 52
Ānanda, 17, 42, 51, 52, 53, 54, 55, 103, 115, 116
Anāthapiṇḍika, 42
Anuruddha, 42
Arahant, Arahat, Arhat, 55, 56
Āryans, 84
Ascetics, 35, 36
Ascetics, Five, 67
Asita, 28
Aśoka, King, 18, 119; greatest Buddhist missionary, 119, 120; his inscriptions, 120, 121
Astrologer, 127
Aśvaghosa, 120
Ātman, 41
Avanti, 25
Avatār, 126

B

Badulla, 126
Beal, 121n.
Beluva, 52, 53
Benares, 27, 39, 40, 67
Bhanda-gama, 54
Bhikkhu, Bhikṣu, 116
Bhikkhu Nārada, 10
Bhikkhuni, Bhikṣuni, 116
Bihar, 43
Bimbisāra, King, 35, 41, 42

Bindusāra, King, 119
'Blacks' of Australia, 84
Bō (Bōdhi)-tree, 36, 37, 63, 67, 118
Brahmā, 37, 38, 68
Brāhman, Oneness with, 47
Brāhmans, 27, 28, 41, 43, 46, 47, 48, 68, 119, 123
Buddha, 9; Ideal, 9; Light of the world, 10; God of Gods, 10; a human being, 10; no contemporary biography of, 23; a mythical figure, 24; dates of birth and death, 24; Public Ministry of, 43; daily habits, 44, 45; his popularity, 45, 46; not radical reformer, 47; old age, 49; kinsmen of, 49; faith in, 52; sickness of, 54; last illness of, 55; last convert, 55; last words, 56; death and burial of, 56; his countless rebirths, 67; his unbelief in Gods, 68; sorrow for him real—not vague *world-sorrow*, 69, 70; his view of individuality, 75; his message—deliverance from rebirth, 95; a joyful message, 99; his 'Path of Escape,' 99; his ministry confined to Kosala and Magadha, 119
Buddha-gayā, 35
Buddhaghosa, 20, 37, 91; on duration of a living being, 76; he defines the word 'Ego,' 79; edited *Pali Tripitaka*, 121; wrote commentaries, 121
Buddhas, Causes of, 66, 68
Bunyan's 'Pilgrim', 34
Burma, 121

C

Cambodia, Buddhism in, 121
Chandragupta, King, 119
Channa (Gotama's servant), 33
Channa (the venerable), his sickness, 97; desire for cessation of existence, 97; his suicide, 97; blameless, 97, 105
China, Buddhism in, 122, 124
Christ Jesus, 112, 115
Chunda, 54
Crawford, Mr., 57

D

Dahlke, Dr. Paul, 34n.; definition of Nirvana, 98
Daladā Māligāwa, 126
Deer Park, 39, 67
Deva, 125, 126
Devadatta, 42, 49
Dēwālas, 126
Dēwatāwō, 126
Dondra, 126

E

Eastern Land, 43
Edinburgh, 44
Egyptians, 84
Ellam, J. E., 79
Exalted One, 38, 50, 51, 52, 53, 54, 55, 56, 67, 105, 106

F

Fa-hian, Fa-Hien, Chinese Pilgrim, 120, 122
Fernando, Sir Marcus, M.D., 57
Franke, 15

G

Ganges, River, 50
Geden, Alfred S., 16n., 18n., 22n.
Geiger, 15
Godhika, 105, 106
Gods, thirty-three, 46
Gooneratne, D. de Silva, 128n.
Gospels, 23
Gotama, 28, 29
Greeks—their influence, 84, 120
Grierson, 15

H

Hackmann, H., 120, 123, 124n., 125n.

Himalayas, 27, 50
Hiranyavati, River, 54
Hiuen-Tsiang, Hiouen-Tsang, 121
Horoscope, 127

I

Indo-Scythian (Kushan) Empire, 120
Isipatana, Deer Park, 39

J

Jesus, 17, 23, 47; teaching of, 64
Jetavana Park, 42

K

Kandy, 126, 128
Kanishka (King), adopted Buddhism, 120
Kanthaka, 33
Kapilavatthu (Kapilavastu), 27, 41, 49
Kapuwās, 126
Kārttikeya (God of War), 126
Kashmir, 120
Kassapa, 40, 41
Kataragama, 126
Keith, A. B., 10n., 15n., 18n., 19n., 20n.
Kisagotami, 32
Koli, 29
Koliyans, 27
Koliyan territory, 33
Korea, Buddhism in, 122
Kosala, 24, 25, 42, 43, 49, 119
Kotigama, 50
Kshatriyas, 27, 46
Kusinara, 45, 49, 54, 56

L

Lankatilaka, 126
Law, B. C., 22n., 121n.
Ledi Sadaw, 20
Levi, 15
Licchavi, 45
London, 44
Lumbini Grove, 28
Luther, 47

M

Macphail, J. M., 120
Magadha, 25, 34, 41, 42, 43, 44, 49, 50, 119

Mahā Cunda, 97
Mahāsanghika, 119
Mahā Vishnu, 126
Mahinda (Mahendra), 121
Mallas, 45, 54
Mallika Queen, 89
Māra, 36, 68, 105, 106
Maya, Lady, 27, 28
Menander (Milinda), King, 77, 120
Mendicants, 33, 41, 46
Merchants, two, 37
Ming-Ti, Emperor, 122
Moggallāna, 41, 43, 90

N

Nadika, 51
Nāgasena, 77, 78, 103, 104; defines *a name*, 77; perception, reason, and soul, 78, 87
Nariman, G. K., 10n., 19n., 23n.
Natha, 126
Nepal, Southern, 27

O

Oldenberg, 15, 39n., 42n., 44, 87n., 111, 113n.
Oudh, 43

P

Pajapati, Lady, 28, 116
Papacy, 47
Pasenadi, 25
Pataligama, Pataliputta (Patna), 50
Pattiny, 126
Pava, 54
Perfect One, 39
Pharisees, 47
Planet god, 127
Plato and Transmigration, 84
Poussin, L. De La Valle, 9n.
Purana, Monk, 22
Pythagoras and Transmigration, 84

R

Rāhula, 29, 32, 42
Raja, 27, 41
Rājagaha, 17, 24, 34, 35, 41, 42, 44, 49, 50, 112
Rajgar, 17, 44

Red Indians, 84
Rhys Davids, Mrs. C. A. F., 11, 15n., 18n., 19n., 21, 37n., 62, 86, 87, 89n., 92, 93n.
Rhys Davids, T. W., 15, 19n., 23n., 42n., 77, 87n.
Roman Catholic Church, 112
Rohini River, 27

S

Sadducees, 47
Sahet Mahet, 44
Śakya clan, 24, 25, 36, 42
Śākyamuni, 9, 11
Śakya Race, 46
Sakyas, Arrogance of, 25, 27
Samana, 46, 47, 68
Sāmmitīya, 119
Sāriputta, 41, 43, 70n., 97
Sarvāstivāda, 119
Sati, 87, 103
Sati Fisher-son, 87
Savatthi, 24, 42, 44
Scythian (Kushan) Empire, 120
Seers' Hill, 105
Shwe Zan Aung, 20
Siam, Buddhism in, 122, 125
Siddhattha, Prince, 28, 29, 31, 34, 35, 39, 40
Silācāra Bhikkhu, 10, 93, 102
Silva, W. A. de, J.P., 127n.
Smith, V. A., 120n.
Stcherbatsky on *Dukkha*, 70
Sthavira, 119
Subhadda, 55
Suddhodana; his marriage, 27, 28, 31, 42
Sumangala, 20
Supreme Teacher, 67, 68
Suriyagoda Sumangala Thera, 64
Sylvain Levi, 19n.

T

Tathāgata, 39, 53, 56, 99
Tathāgatas, 11
Tibet, Buddhism in, 122, 124
Tissa, Monk, 18
Turner, 15

U

Uddaka, 35
United Provinces, 27

Universal Monarch, 28
Upāli, 17, 42
Upavattana, 54
Uruvelā, 35, 40, 41, 67

V

Vallee Poussin, L. De La, 9n.
Vaṃsas, 25
Vasavha Khattiya, 25
Veluvana, 42
Vesālī, 45, 52, 54
Vihāra, 126

Visākhā, 42
Vishnu, 11, 126

W

Wessamuny, 127
Western Hindustan, 43, 44
Warren, 44n., 66n., 71, 89n., 102n.,
    113n., 116

Y

Yamaka, 72
Yasa, 39, 40
Yaśodharā, 29, 42
Yoruba Negroes, 84

APPENDIX III

INDEX OF SUBJECTS

A

Abhidhamma, 19
Abhidhamma-Pitaka, 16, 17, 62
Ahimsawardana, 57
All-Soul (*Brahman-Ātman*), 68
Almsgiving, importance of, 89
Anatta, 66, 70, 91, 101, 107
Anguttara-Nikāya, 10, 16, 66
Anichcha, Anicca, 66, 71
Arahantship, 52, 55
Aryan India, 43
Āryan Truths, Four, 51
Asia, the masses of, 10
Atasil, 117
Atmā, 101
Awareness, 74
Āyatanas, twelve, 73

B

Bali, Buddhism in, 122
Bali Ceremonies, 127
Bhikku, 54, 56, 64, 87, 103, 105, 106
Bhikkuni, 116
Birth, Old age, Death, 68, 69, 71, 95
Bon, 124
Brahmajāla-Sutta, 99
Brahman-Ātman, not mentioned by Buddha, 68n.; absorption into, 85
Brahmanism, 47, 119, 124
Buddhism, 9; *Buddhism in a Nutshell*, 10; wholly unique, 10; primitive, 61; a devitalized thing, 62; historical development of, 119; a sect of Brahmanism, 119; early dissensions of, 119; Four Early Schools of *Mahāsanghika, Sthavira, Sarvāstivāda*, and *Sāmmitiya*, 119;

Buddhism—*contd.*
expansion under Asoka, 120; degeneracy of, 121; influence of Muslim Invasion on, 121; popularity of, 121; decaying, 121; in Ceylon, 121, 125; in Burma, 121, 125; in Mongolia, 124
Buddhism as a Religion, 123; it is not a gospel for the poor, 123; tolerance of, 123, 125; a religion of magic, 124; Polytheistic, 124; in Tibet corrupt, 124; in Hinayana, 125
Buddhist Annual of Ceylon, 79, 88
Buddhist Chronicle, 93n.
Buddhist definition of *an individual*, 80
Buddhist Doctrine of Man, 71
Buddhist India, 19n.
Buddhist (modern) analysis of man, 79
Buddhist Philosophy, 15n., 19n.
Buddhist Psychology, 74n., 75, 86n., 87n.
Buddhists, 9; orthodox, 20; Buddhas, 10; Bodhisattvas, 10; Bliss perpetual, 10; Buddhist Pantheon, 10; Buddhist monks, 10
Buddhists' horror of Eternal Life, 99
Burmese Views, 20

C

Canon, Buddhist, 15, 18, 19, 22, 86
Canon, Pali, 20
Cause, First, 88
Celebates, 47
Cetanā, 64
Ceylon Buddhism, 120, 121; Its conflicting beliefs, 126; Its Hindu gods, 126; Its *Kapuism*, 126; Its worship of *Vishnu*, 126;

Ceylon Buddhism—*contd.*
Perahera ceremonies, 126; Its *Grahaism*, 127; Its Demonism, 127, 128; *Bali* ceremonies, 127; *Pirit* and *Piritnool*, 128; Statistics, 129
Ceylon Buddhists and flesh eating, 56, 57
Ceylon Commentary, 20
Charms, *Hooniyan*, 128
Christian Gospels, 23
Christianity, 125
Cinema picture, 80, 81
Compendium of Philosophy, 20n.
Confucianist, 124
Consciousness, definition of, 73, 74; (*viññāna*), 86; in relation to rebirth, 86; in relation to *Nirvana*, 103; not reborn unchanged, 103; (*viññāna*) not the soul, 103; and the *chain of causality*, 103, 104, 105; Transmigration of, denied, 104; nevertheless connecting link in *Karmic Series*, 105; utterly ceased to live, 106
Constituents of being, 63
Council, 17, 112
Councils: Buddhist, 119; Kanishka's at Jalandhara, 120
Creator defined, 88
Cullavagga, 16, 95

D

Daśa-sīla, 113
Death, Indian view of, 68; kindly, beneficent, 68
Deliverance, way of, 68
Demonism, 127, 128
Dependent Origination defined, 88
Devas, 125
Dhammapada, 11, 17, 96
Dhammasangani, 17
Dhātukathā, 17
Dharma (element), 73, 74, 81
Dhātus, Eighteen, 74, 101, 102, 103
Digha-Nikāya, 16, 86, 99
Disciples, first sixty, 40
Doctrine, Buddha's, 39, 55
Doctrine, Buddhist, 61
Doctrine of Man, Buddhist, 71

Dolla, 128
Dukkha, 66, 70, 97
Dysentery, 54

E

Eastern Memory, 21
Eating of flesh not forbidden, 56
Ego, 63
Element, An, a point in time space, 81, 102
Elements of Being, perpetually in a state of commotion, 97; quieted by wisdom, 101
Elements of existence defined, 81
Enlightenment, supreme knowledge, 37, 56, 90
E.R.E., 84n., 121n., 122n., 125n.
Esoteric Doctrine, 53
Eternal Salvation, 10, 99
Ethics, 61
Exorcism, 121
Exoteric Doctrine, 53

F

Four Signs, the, 28, 29, 30, 31
Fruitless Suffering, 35, 36

G

Goal, the, 63
God, 68
God Supreme, 10
Gotama the Man, 12, 62
Gotama's Teachers, 35; His great discovery, 36, 37
Grahaism, 127
Great Decease, the Book of the, 49
Greek Text of New Testament, 19

H

Hīnayāna Buddhism, 9, 15, 120, 125
Hindu Theory of Soul and *Karma*, 85
Home Leaving, 30

I

Ignorance, 95, 96, 98, 101
Impermanence, 66, 70, 71, 72, 107
Individual stream, 80
Individuality, illusion of, 95
Intoxications, 55

Invocations, 128
Islām, 15

J

Japan, Buddhism in, 124
Jātaka, 17, 71
Java, Buddhism in, 122
Jhānas (ecstatic trances) described, 102, 103, 107

K

Kaleidoscope, 80
Kamma (Karma), 63, 83, 93
Kanishka, Council of, 18, 120
Kapuism, 126
Karma survives death of body, 83; not peculiar to Buddhism, 83; Hindu doctrine, 83; probable origin of doctrine, 85; an Ethical theory, 85; only persistent reality in man, 86; defined, 86; defined more fully, 89, 90
Kathāvatthu, 17
Khandhakas, 16
Khandhas (Skandhas), 79, 93
Khuddaka-Nikāya, 17
King Milinda, Questions of, 15, 77, 87, 120
Korea (Buddhism in), 122
Kosala, dialect of, 21

L

Lalita Vistara, 23n.
Lamaism, 124
Law, Impersonal, Mechanical, 37
Lay-followers, 37, 116
Life, a spectre of horror, 68
Living Being, what constitutes, 66

M

Magadha, dialect of, 21
Mahāparinibbāna-Sutta, 49, 113n.
Mahasanghika, 119
Mahāsangīti or 'Great Council', 17
Mahāvagga, 16, 118n.
Mahāyāna, 9, 120
Mahāyānists, 9, 124
Majjhima-Nikāya, 16, 21n., 87n., 96
Man, his own Refuge, 53
Mantra, 128

Manual of Buddhism, 19n., 62
Matter *(rupa)*, 72; (1) objective sense-data; (2) sense organs; matter without substance, 72
Memoirs, 26
Merit (Religious), 118
Message, Joyful, 98, 99
Metaphysics, 17, 61
Middle Way, 39
Milinda-pañha, The, 15, 77, 87, 120
Mind less permanent than body, 75, 76
Mirror of Truth, 51, 52
Muhammadan invasion in Java, 122
Muhammadanism, 125.

N

Nāma-rūpa, 72, 88
Nat worship, 125
New Testament, 15, 19
Nibbāna (Nirvāna), 64, 98
Nirodha, 102
Nirvāna, 9, 47, 55, 61, 63; a negative, not a positive conception, 95; a living experience, 96, 98; further defined, 106; at least inanimate, 106; ineffable bliss, 106; practical directions for attainment of, 107, 115
Noble Eightfold Path, 52, 64, 67, 107
Noble Eightfold Path, The, 102
Non-Ego, 66, 70, 71, 72, 102
Nuns, The order of *(Bhikkhuni-Sangha)*, Buddha strongly opposed to, 115; Ānanda's pleading for, 115; Buddha yielded to pleading of Mahapajapati, 116

O

Oral Tradition, 23
Order of Monks, 39, 47, 52, 53
Order, the *(Bhikkhu-Sangha)*, 111; Founded by Buddha, 111; Laws in *Patimokkha*, 111; Buddha, master of, 111; not a compact organization, 112; left without a Head, 112; early schisms, 112; entry into, in theory, open to any one, 112; Persons excluded

Order—*contd.*
 from, 112; Initiation Ceremonies, 113; four great prohibitions, 113; the ten commandments (*Dasa-sila*), 113;
 Rules regarding property, 114;
 Full and New Moon day
 meetings, 114, 115; regular acts
 of public worship, 115, 116, 119
Order, the, faith in, 52

P

Pabbajja ceremony, 112
Pachchaya-satti, 92
Pali Language, 15
Pali Literature, History of, 22
Pali Patakas, 9, 11, 15, 16, 17, 46,
 49, 121, 125, 127
Pansil, 117
Pantheon, 10
Papacy, 47
Parinibbāna-Sutta, 11
Parinirvana, 56; What is it? 98;
 Is it everlasting unconscious
 existence? 99; defined, 100;
 remainderlessness, 101, 106
Parivāra, 16
Pataliputta, Council of, 18
Path, the, 53, 63, 101
Patisanvedanaka, 64
Paṭṭhāna, 17
Paṭicca-samuppāda, 88
Pātimokkha, commentary on, 16,
 111
Pavāraṇā, 115
Perahera Ceremonies, 126
Perfected Saint like a burnt-out
 lamp, 100
Permanence, 70
Personal identity, no continuous,
 76, 77, 81
Pessimism, 68
Philosophy of Buddhism, 61
Pilgrimage (*Samsāra*), 69
'*Points of Controversy*,' 19n., 20
Pork, 54, 56
Poson, 57
Poya days, 114
Primitive Buddhism, 61
Prapti, 80
Psychology, 61
Pudgala, 101

Puggala-Paññatti, 17
Purgatory, 51

Q

Qurān, 15

R

Rainy Season, 44
Rainy Season (*Vassa*), 52
Rajagaha, Council of, 112
Rebirth ended, 51, 54
Rebirth, peculiar to Buddhism, 83;
 and Karma, 83; in absence of
 soul, 86; Nagasena's definition,
 87, 88; without transmigration
 and evasion of justice, 88; mode
 of, not explained by the Buddha,
 91; a dogma to be accepted by
 faith, 91; Buddhaghosa's at-
 tempt at explanation, 92; Mrs.
 Rhys Davids' comment, 92, 93;
 Silacara Bhikkhu's attempt at
 explanation, 93; influenced by
 dying thought, 94, 103, 104, 105
Refuges, The Three, 111
Religious Mendicancy; popularity
 of, 46
Repeaters, 21
Revelation, 10
Rock Edicts of Aśoka, 19
Rūpa, 72, 79, 80, 88

S

Sacred Truth of Suffering, 39
S.B.B., 42n., 49n., 51n., 52n., 54n.,
 55n., 56n., 87n., 94n., 99n.,
 100n., 103n., 107n.
Sacrificial System, 48
Saints, calmness of, 97
Saivism in Java, 122
Sakya, 12, 15n., 18n., 21n., 56n.,
 62, 104n.
Sala Grove, 54
Samana Movement, 46, 47
Sammaditthi, 64
Sāmmitīya, 119
Samsāra, 69, 88
Samyutta-Nikāya, 16, 69, 75, 86n.
 95
Sankhāra, 73, 79
Sangha, 50
Sankhar-Uppatti Sutta, 94n.
Saññā, 73
Sanskrit Buddhism, 10n., 23n.

Sarvāstivāda, 119

Schools, Buddhist; *Mahāyāna* and *Hinayāna*, 9, 11, 120, 124, 125

Self-torture, 36

Series, An Infinite and Eternal, 86

Shintoist, 124

Shiva Cycle, 9

Sil, 117

Sinhalese Buddhist, 125, 126, 127, 128

Skandhas, 72; Five, 63

Social Reformer, 47

Sons of noble houses, 40, 41, 48

Sorrow or Ill, 66, 68, 70, 71

Sorrow, Universal, 69, 71; no escape from, 69; of gods, 69; sorrow all-pervading, 95, 99

Sotāpanna, 113

Soul, Indian view of, 82

Soul, only a name, not a reality, 66, 82, 104

Sources of Buddhism, 15

Spells, 128

Sthavira, 119

Subordinate to monks, 116

Suffering, noble truths of, 39, 51

Suffering, Universality of, 67, 68, 69, 70, 71, 99

Sumatra, Buddhism in, 122

Summum bonum, 47, 61

Supreme will, 88

Sutta-Pitaka, 16, 62

Sutta-Vibhanga, 16

Suttanta, 50, 86

T

Tantrism, 121, 124

Taoist, 124

Temptation, Gotama's, 36

The Central Conception of Buddhism, 70n., 73n., 74, 81n., 106n.

The Four Signs: Sickness, Disease, Old Age, Death, 28, 68, 69, 71

The Four Visions, 30, 31

The Order of Laymen and Women (*Upāsakā* and *Upāsikā*), 116; essential to existence of order of mendicants, 117; vows of *Pansil* or *Atasil*, 117; no regular religious gatherings of, 117; Passion for acquiring merit, 118

The Three Characteristics, 62, 70, 71

The Times of Ceylon, 57

Tradition, Oral, 19, 21, 22

Traditionalists, Buddhists are, 62

Transitoriness, 70, 72

Transmigration, 32, 51, 54, 88

Transmigration of the Soul, 83; wide-spread belief in, 83, 84; African theories, 83, 84; theories of Red Indians and Blacks, 84; Egyptians and Greeks, 84; not held by early *Aryans*, 84; not found in *Vedas*, 84; first found in *Upanishads*, 84; Buddhists' working theory of life, 93, 104

Tripitaka, 15, 61, 91, 121

Triple Basket, 15

Truth, Faith in, 52, 53

Truth, Mirror of, 51, 52

Truths, The Four Noble, 54

Truths, The Three Universal, 66, 71

U

Universe, 67

Upanishads, 84

Upāsakā, 116, 117

Upasampadā Ceremony, 113

Upāsikā, 116

V

Vaisali, 17

Vassa (*Was*), 43, 52, 115

Vedanā, 73n.

Vedas, 21, 84

Vedic Culture, 43

Vibhanga Sutta, 16

Vibhanga, 17

Vinaya-Pitaka, 16, 19, 62

Viññāna, Vijñāna, 73n., 86, 87, 104

Visuddhimagga, The, 15, 63, 79, 91

Vihara, 126

W

Wesak, 57

Wheel of the Law, 39

Writing, the art of, 18

Wheel of life, The, 98

Y

Yamaka, 17